STRIVING TOGETHER PUBLICATIONS

CHURCH STILL WORKS

An In-Depth Study of the Practices

and Potential of Twenty-first

Century Local Churches

PAUL CHAPPELL
& CLAYTON REED

The Inside Story from a National Survey
of Independent Baptist Churches

Striving Together Publications
4020 E. Lancaster Blvd.
Lancaster, CA 93535
800.201.7748

Cover design by Andrew Jones
Layout by Craig Parker
Edited by Cary Schmidt
Editing assistance by Sarah Michael, Amanda Michael, and Monica Bass
Special thanks to our review team and proofreaders

The contents of this book are the result of twenty-five years of spiritual growth in life and ministry. The authors and publication team have given every effort to give proper credit to quotes and thoughts that are not original with the authors. It is not our intent to claim originality with any quote or thought that could not readily be tied to an original source.

ISBN 978-1-59894-079-4

Printed in the United States of America

FROM PAUL CHAPPELL

To the Baptist church planter who goes to a place by faith, wins souls, endures trials, and proves God's plan—the local church.

FROM CLAYTON REED

To my fathers.

My grandfather, Rowe Burton Reed, faithful pastor, church planter, and patriarch through sixty-two years of ministry.

My dad, Samuel Kent Reed, loving husband, beloved father, dedicated pastor and Bible teacher, unsung behind-the-scenes hero.

Two men after God's own heart.

TABLE OF CONTENTS

FROM PAUL CHAPPELL

Special thanks to Brother Cary Schmidt for all your help in bringing this project together during and incredibly busy season in our own local church ministry.

I also wish to thank Dr. Don Sisk, Dr. R.B. Ouellette, Evangelist Paul Schwanke, Pastor Kurt Skelly, Dr. Eldon Martens, Pastor Mark Irmler, Evangelist Mike Gass, Dr. Bob Smith, Dr. John Goetsch, Dr. Mark Rasmussen, John Teichert, Pastor Stephen Chappell, Pastor Rob Badger, Pastor Troy Dorrell, Pastor Josh Teis, Pastor Alan Fong, Pastor Chris Edwards, and Pastor Mike Norris, for their insight and suggestions on this project.

Finally, I wish to acknowledge the valiant efforts of Rob and Tina Badger in planting the Victory Baptist Church in North Hollywood. While some visit from conference to conference, church planters like the Badgers still visit lost people door to door. These church planters are fulfilling God's plan by faith, and their efforts inspire us!

FROM CLAYTON REED

This page—the last written—may be the most important, because it acknowledges the fact that, if not for the family, friends, and coworkers named below, none of the others would have been possible.

To my wife, Heather, and kids—Jack, Josh, Eric, Matthew, Tyler, and Abby—for putting up with the project over the course of a year. Apart from your patience, understanding, and encouragement, I could never have finished this work.

To Zack, for the seemingly endless hours you spent looking at numbers with me, and to Lindsay, for keeping everything in order while the project was ongoing. Your insight, skill, and dedication not only helped this train run on time, but actually kept it on the tracks.

To Mark, for helping it all make sense on paper. From my stream-of-consciousness writing, you drew out precisely what I wanted to say.

To Pastor Smith, for your counsel in approaching the research and your feedback during the early writing. Your wisdom and experience sharpened my focus and deepened my insight.

And to all the pastors who took the time to complete the research. Without your contribution, there would have been no data, no insights, no conclusions, and no opportunity for others to be blessed by your adventures in ministry.

FROM PAUL CHAPPELL

It was the subject of local church planting and development that first allowed me to cross paths with Clayton Reed. He, like many other independent Baptists, has been burdened to encourage and help the work of local church ministry, one church at a time. I am grateful for the opportunity to work with Clayton on this project. He has travelled the world and invested much of his time, heart, and resources into helping missionaries and national pastors to plant local churches. I admire his passion for the local church and identify with his desire to encourage independent Baptists.

With that desire in mind, we met and began to discuss and pray about local church planting and development. Clayton began to use his mix of spiritual gifts to study, travel, interview, and prepare much of the material you are about to read. I am especially appreciative for his willingness to fund an objective comprehensive study of the independent Baptist churches of our nation.

We have seen publications which record data from a small segment of independent Baptist churches, and we are interested in these reports. But, our desire was for a broader perspective—to learn where our churches are, spiritually, philosophically, regionally, and numerically in order to "strengthen the things that remain."

There are a few things you should know about this book.

First, our primary concern is understanding and helping local independent Baptist churches. If we use the word "movement," we speak of God's moving on the hearts of men to plant and build up churches. Our subject is not "fundamentalism." We understand there are groups that are non-Baptist yet hold to basic fundamental Bible doctrine. We appreciate their love for Christ. But this is not a study of interdenominational proportions. The local Baptist church is being used of God worldwide as you will read in this book. Though there are many places we must still reach, God's plan is working very well, and the objective research validates this conclusion.

Many modern Christians are choosing to "go around" the local church, and some authors are subverting the local church. We are concerned with this approach because our experience with local church ministry is quite different than that of these authors. Granted, they have apparently experienced and studied some weak examples—as there are plenty to study. As a result, some are encouraging believers to abandon the local church completely (they refer to it as the institutional church) and to just "be the church" with a very nondescript, non-structured sort of "worship" that finds no real basis in Scripture. We believe that this is an unbiblical over-reaction that is harmful to God's people. Yes, there are problems in churches because they are made up of people, but God's plan and intent for the local church function is clear in Scripture and should be embraced with full faith and assurance.

Next, you need to know we are thankful for the men throughout history who have stood against compromise and have stood for soulwinning, biblical separation, and church planting to build this unaffiliated, independent group of churches. They came from different molds. Some came out of denominations which were compromising. Others were saved within independent Baptist churches.

This study is not in any way about criticizing them or "reinventing" the churches they have established. While we will speak about excellence and methodology, our belief is that the strength of independent Baptists is not found in the reinvention of God's model, but in the duplication of it! We are committed to *duplicating* God's New Testament pattern of the local church. We have no desire merely to write a secular or corporate perspective of popular church growth practices, as so many in the "seeker-sensitive" church movement have done. We desire to lift up the principles of God's Word that He is still blessing in local churches today, and to encourage you to embrace and practice them fervently.

We have all seen periodic pettiness and weaknesses in our ranks (as did the first century churches). When this occurs, we must pray, humble ourselves, and grow personally. Yet we know where we stand and have no intention of re-aligning ourselves doctrinally or philosophically with other movements or "-isms." We believe that our churches are founded with the right body of pure doctrine and the right philosophical principles. In fact, it is for the preservation and propagation of these doctrines and principles that we write this book.

I am intrigued by some independent Baptists who speak glowingly of groups outside of Baptist circles, only to find out later, there are sin problems, jealousy, and divisive issues in every "group." These are people problems, not Baptist problems. In reality, local independent Baptist churches are truly making a dramatic difference for eternity. In fact, you will see that the lack of denominational organization or funding processes has not diminished the work of independent Baptist missions and has actually helped the churches to maintain doctrinal integrity.

Finally, we are *for* you. If you pastor a church, serve faithfully in a church, or care about revival, we are for you. If you believe we must increase our efforts to share the Gospel, we are for you. If you desire for your church to become healthier and stronger, we are for you. If you long for lives to be changed by the power of the Gospel in your local church, we are for you. If you are in the trenches planting a church, we salute you. If you are for the local church, we are for you.

The spirit of these pages is positive, uplifting, prayerful, and encouraging! We thank God for missions-supporting, faith-believing, soulwinning Baptists who would rather make a difference than spend idle time biting and devouring others through gossip, online chat, and conjecture.

Perhaps you have sensed the increasing animosity toward conservative Christians in America. For example, in an article defending homosexual marriage, the editor of *Newsweek* recently wrote, "…to argue that something is so because it is in the Bible, is more than intellectually bankrupt."[2]

We also see the continuing moral decline in our country. Just prior to this writing, the President of the United States lifted the ban on giving federal money to international groups that promote abortion. Amazingly, in the midst of a financial crisis, our nation is providing funds to help other countries murder their unborn!

We believe now is the time, more than ever, for a resurgence of local churches to reach out with the Gospel and stand up for the faith. We believe the *size* of your church does not have to affect the *health* and *reach* of your church. Every independent Baptist church, in every location and of every size, must be challenged to capture their area for Christ and to participate in planting new local churches! To that end, we pray for you, and we offer these pages for your encouragement. May God bless you, and may your local church continue to do God's work for His glory.

Paul Chappell
Lancaster, California
March 2009

FROM CLAYTON REED

Growing up as an independent Baptist, I remember hearing amazing stories about vibrant, evangelistic churches across America and their dynamic leaders. I was pleased to know that most of those congregations were independent Baptist churches that believed and practiced the essential biblical doctrines of the Christian faith.

More recently, I read with great interest *Outreach* magazine's list of the 100 largest, fastest-growing churches. I was distressed to realize it was practically devoid of independent Baptist congregations. Only one made the list—a far cry from the day when independent Baptist congregations led the way in America. I began to wonder about the future of this local church movement. Were we just another man-made movement that once showed promise but then faded into irrelevance and obscurity? Was our movement like a patient on life support—propped up in bed, kept alive mechanically but sick in spirit, waiting to die?

Or was there something more to it than a mere "movement"?

Because of this, I wrestled with the thought that perhaps God was no longer interested in giving growth to our churches. Could it be that some generations were not meant to have growing churches? How many independent Baptist churches were still alive and well and making a difference?

I decided to see what I could learn about the state of the independent Baptist churches of our nation. I began asking different pastors if they had any statistical information about who we are and how effective our churches are. It became apparent that most of the information we had about our types of churches was either limited in scope or anecdotal and unsubstantiated.

With these thoughts in mind, I sat down with a new acquaintance— Pastor Paul Chappell. We met in his office on the West Coast. After hearing my concerns and thoughts, Pastor Chappell pulled out a piece of paper and began to sketch out a diagram of what might be referred to as the fundamental, independent Baptist movement—the society of independent Baptists that hold to pure doctrine and conservative biblical living.

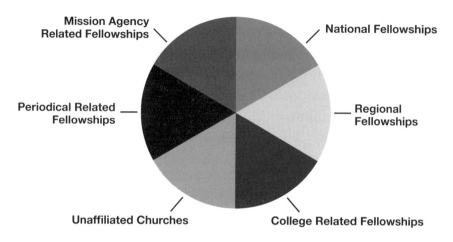

Mission Agency Related Fellowships

National Fellowships

Periodical Related Fellowships

Regional Fellowships

Unaffiliated Churches

College Related Fellowships

Proportions are not intended to be accurate.

Pastor Chappell explained that independent Baptists are a large group that contains dozens of subsets. Some of those subsets are affiliated with Bible colleges, others with papers and publications. Some are part of nationwide conferences, while others identify more readily with particular doctrines or geographies. Some of the subsets cross over into other subsets. A significant number of congregations—in good independent tradition—identify with no subsets.

Pastor Chappell and I talked a long time about the evolution of the movement. When we were done, I was very grateful for the insight I had received, but I still could not quantify much about the state of local independent Baptist churches in America.

After many discussions with Pastor Chappell and others, I decided to commission the first nationwide survey of independent Baptist churches. Conducting the research posed many challenges. The biggest obstacle was our lack of expertise in developing research. No organization within our independent Baptist circles had ever conducted a survey like the one I was proposing. So we made a decision to partner with a well-known Christian research organization that could assist us in developing the survey and interpreting the results. Because this organization has conducted literally thousands of surveys, it had the expertise we needed to develop a research project that would produce statistically reliable information. We also wanted an independent set of eyes to review the research data and draw out unbiased conclusions. I know that I am quite biased by my love for independent Baptist churches, and I wanted to know the real story—good or bad.

Pastor Chappell and I hoped the survey would quantify the growth trends, size, habits, and priorities of the independent Baptist churches in America. More than that, we hoped the survey would validate that local church ministry is still alive and thriving as God promised. We were hoping to verify that our churches were more than a dying movement, but indeed a God-blessed institution moving forward. We also wanted to know what churches were being blessed and which biblical principles they followed most fervently.

After much planning and discussions with key pastors across the United States, we mailed the survey to 13,719 independent Baptist churches. Over the course of the following two months, we received approximately 550 qualified responses from a broad spectrum of congregations—those from many various subsets of independent Baptists. Many other churches responded, but their data had to be disqualified because the information provided was incomplete. To give you an idea of how significant this sample size was, polling organizations can reliably predict how 140 million Americans will vote based on a mere 1,300 interviews. Since we mailed our surveys to every possible congregation, there was in effect no margin of error in the findings.

After the responses were tabulated, the research organization analyzed the results and gave us approximately ninety pages of graphs, information, and observations. Some of the information was encouraging and showed us that God is still powerfully at work in our local churches. We did, however, see that in some areas the findings were negative and did not bode well for our future if changes are not made.

My sincere desire is for independent Baptists to have a vibrant future because I believe them to be the most biblically accurate representation of the local church of Jesus Christ on this planet today. While some have left our conservative, biblical philosophy in search of "greener pastures," I am determined to walk the same biblically sound paths my fathers walked. I have been an independent Baptist my entire life and intend to remain so, but I am not willing to close my eyes to our shortcomings. A man-made movement may be relegated to the dustbin of history, but local New Testament churches are still God's plan for changing lives today.

All across this nation there are healthy, thriving, local independent Baptist churches that God is genuinely blessing. In the coming pages, I believe you will be stirred and challenged by the research we have conducted. I believe you will be greatly encouraged about the future of the local, New Testament church.

A pastor in England in the early 1900s, became concerned about the effectiveness and spiritual climate of his church in his day. He saw Christians losing sight of their original commission, and in response he wrote:

> I feel a commissioning to work under God for the revival of this branch of His Church—careless of my own reputation; indifferent to the comments of older and jealous men. I am thirty-six. If I am to serve God in this way, I must no longer shrink from the task—but do it.
>
> I have examined my heart for ambition. I am certain it is not there. I hate the criticism I shall evoke and the painful chatter of people. Obscurity, quiet browsing among books, and the service of simple people is my taste—but by the will of God, this is my task....
>
> Bewildered and unbelieving, I hear the voice of God saying to me, "I want to sound the note through you." O God, did ever an apostle shrink from his task more? I dare not say "no" but, like Jonah, I would fain [wish to] run away.
>
> God help me. God help me.[1]

I identify with the spirit of this burdened pastor. My desire is to see independent Baptists return with a new zeal to our real work and our biblical roots. We must return to our mission.

Because of my age and relative lack of experience, I felt I needed a respected partner to help tell this story. My colleague in this endeavor is no stranger to independent Baptist churches, and the story of his ministry is simply thrilling. Pastor Paul Chappell started the Lancaster

Baptist Church in 1986 in the high desert of California with a small group of people. Some twenty-three years later, the church averages more than 4,700 in weekly attendance and baptizes over 600 new converts each year. Far more important than the numbers, however, is the thriving, healthy spirit of soulwinning, discipleship, and biblical maturity that is developing in the lives of thousands of young Christians at Lancaster Baptist. This church says to all of us, "God still can."

Our prayer is that this book will be an encouragement to pastors and layman alike and show us all how God still blesses and uses local church ministry! May God grant us a new day of effectiveness in winning souls, making disciples, and planting local churches for His glory.

Clayton Reed
Arlington, Texas
February 2009

INTRODUCTION

I s the local church dead? Is it a failed relic of history? Is it nothing more than a flawed monument to irrelevance and man-made traditions? Many would have us think so.

Everywhere you turn, sources are predicting the extinction of the local church as we know it. They are declaring that local churches are dying and denominations are failing. Christians and non-Christians alike are heralding an American mass exodus from church. From the non-Christians we hear that church is impractical and unable to meet the social ills and needs of society.

Coming from a secular viewpoint, in his March 13, 2009 column in *The Wall Street Journal,* W. Bradford Wilcox begins by stating, "Secularism seems to be on the march in America...the number of Americans claiming no religion now stands at 15%, up from 8% in 1990 and 2% in 1962." His argument, put simply, is that the expansion of the government sector to offer cradle-to-grave social services contributes to the secularization of the society. With the growth of a welfare state and the postponement of marriage and parenthood for many young adults comes a decreased motivation to commit to a local church. Wilcox writes:

> The secular tide appears to be running strongest among young Americans. Religious attendance among those 21 to 45 years old is at its lowest level in decades, according to Princeton sociologist Robert Wuthnow. Only 25% of young adults now attend services regularly, compared with about one-third in the early 1970s.
>
> The most powerful force driving religious participation down is the nation's recent retreat from marriage, Mr. Wuthnow notes. Nothing brings women and especially men into the pews like marriage and parenthood, as they seek out the religious, moral and social support provided by a congregation upon starting a family of their own. But because growing numbers of young adults are now postponing or avoiding marriage and childbearing, they are also much less likely to end up in church on any given Sunday. Mr. Wuthnow estimates that America's houses of worship would have about six million more regularly attending young adults if today's young men and women started families at the rate they did three decades ago.

From some Christians we hear—*revolt*! Church is obsolete and ineffective—irrelevant. Don't *go* to church, *be* the church. Author and Christian researcher George Barna essentially predicts the demise of the local church. Though he was reached through a local church and has spent much of his life pioneering the "seeker-sensitive" church movement, he now rejects the institution of the local church. He and his co-authors write against the local church and essentially encourage Christians to leave their churches. He states: "Millions of believers have moved beyond the established church…and [have] chosen to be the church instead."[1] A chief researcher and promoter of the market-driven church now declares that his invention was ineffective, and he equates the flawed experiment with the failure of God's institution.

While we might agree that many mainline denominations have failed as a result of years of compromise—more and more, Barna and others are lumping *all churches* into a category of outdated, ineffective, unfruitful models of ecclesiastical liturgy and tradition.

The claim of these authors and researchers is that there is "another side"—a higher level of personal worship and a lifestyle of complete devotion to Jesus Christ that excludes local church involvement. While, indeed, our Christian lifestyle is to be one of complete devotion, that does not exclude us from the local church participation that Christ clearly intends for His followers. A life of full devotion is not incompatible with the biblical model of local church ministry—it is essential to it.

Is the local church dead or dying? Are these voices accurate? Are they presenting the entire story? Are we indeed seeing the demise of local church ministry through the forsaking of an institution for a more self-centered worship? What about the promise of Christ and the overwhelming instruction of the New Testament to local churches of believers?

There is much more to this story...

Research just in—according to the study contained in this book, there is a host of believers and local churches that never bought into the "seeker-sensitive" movement.

Enter—thousands upon thousands of healthy, thriving New Testament churches which popular Christian "pollsters turned prophets" have not visited or researched.

Cue the good news—these local bodies are reaching the lost, discipling new believers, teaching the Word, supporting missions around the world, ministering to communities, meeting spiritual and social needs, planting new local churches, and encouraging new life and growing faith all over the world.

No, the self-centered "Christian revolution" is not the only alternative to dead orthodoxy. It's time to see the research that popular researchers haven't seen. In those well-known words of Paul Harvey, it's time to hear "the rest of the story."

The purpose of this book is to state an objective, substantiated case that God's plan for the local church has not failed. We will highlight and study those biblical practices that God is blessing in healthy local churches around the world. These chapters present a well-documented, biblical approach to effective local church life—God's plan for every Christian.

This study also reveals, however, that when certain imbalances occur within local churches, their effectiveness diminishes—even when they possess a pure doctrinal position. Health and growth in a local church is the product of both pure doctrine and biblical practice. This book focuses on the practices that will better align local churches with scriptural admonitions. Much as the Lord Jesus called the seven churches of Asia Minor back to their first love and founding principles, may the Holy Spirit call us back to biblical models for local church ministry.

Allow us to make a few quantifying statements before you read further. First, while we believe that the statistics and surveys assembled in this book are accurate, we do not presume to imply that they are definitively certain. Second, as independent Baptists, we are not in competition with one another, other groups, or denominations. The data shared should be viewed in that light. Third, we do not intend to imply that numerical growth always equals a healthy church. There are thousands of small, healthy churches across the country pastored by faithful men of God. And over the centuries, some of the greatest Christians in full-time and lay ministry have come from these types of churches. We pray that this book will greatly encourage these faithful pastors and church families. And finally, while we write much about "what works" in local church ministry, please understand—we do not practice these principles because "they work"—we practice them because they are biblical.

The local church of Jesus Christ is alive and well, and it is the only hope of doing God's work God's way. It is God's plan for the evangelization of the world and the edification of His people. Much of our New Testament is written to local churches of the first century, and in these epistles we are given doctrine, polity, and practice for the daily needs of our local churches to this day.

Thousands of local churches are growing, thriving, and seeing lasting life-change just as Jesus promised. And by *church* we refer to what God's Word refers to when it mentions the word *church*—local, called-out assemblies of organized bodies of believers—bodies that have pastors, deacons, times of assembly and worship, Bible teaching and preaching, offerings, ministries, and missionaries. We mean modern day examples of exactly what we read about in the book of Acts and in many of the New Testament Epistles. This is the institution that Jesus Christ loves and for which He gave His life, and He is still working powerfully in these local bodies of believers all over the globe.

Man-made movements have failed. Denominations have declined. Liturgy, traditions of men, and religiosity have left mankind searching. Prognosticators decry the church (as *they* know it) to be declining and dying. Schisms and "-isms" have come to naught. But God's local church remains.

In a day when pastors are running to and fro to learn the newest way to please seekers, or when Christians are being called to revolt against God's institution, we are secure and confident in God's original blueprint for local church ministry. And we believe the primary aim of a godly pastor and church family is to please Jesus Christ, not to please man or self.

May we, once again, follow God's plan and give our lives to that which He loves—the local, New Testament church in its most tangible, functioning, practical, and biblical form.

By the title of this book—*Church Still Works*—we refer to our passionate belief that God still blesses and uses healthy, local churches all over the world. We pray for a revival of Christians who will believe God's Word and align themselves with God's institution once again. We pray for a renewal of pastors who will take their eyes off *movements* and refocus on the *mission* of their own local church. We pray for a renewed and energetic effort toward planting and establishing local churches all over the world.

The local church is Christ's institution—His plan still works.

1

ARE WE MAKING A DIFFERENCE?

W ho are the independent Baptists? Where did we come from? How are our churches doing, and what's ahead for future leaders?

In the next four chapters we will introduce the independent Baptist church movement of the United States and highlight a nationwide survey conducted by an independent research group. We will briefly examine our past and then begin to study the state of our churches in the present.

The news is both encouraging and challenging! Many things are going well in the independent Baptist churches of our nation. God is still blessing His plan for the local church. At the same time, many things can be strengthened, and there is much work for us to accomplish together.

THIS BAND OF BROTHERS

We few, we happy few, we band of brothers;
For he to-day that sheds his blood with me
Shall be my brother; be he ne'er so vile,
—WILLIAM SHAKESPEARE,
St. Crispen's Day Speech, "Henry V"

Independent Baptist is not a denomination, but rather a family—a band of brothers. Like most brothers, we disagree with each other from time to time. But we also share a deep family bond as brothers in Christ. We are bound together by a zeal for the pure Gospel and a passion for precious souls and are dispatched as ambassadors of the King to make disciples of all the nations.

But who are we, this band of brothers? Our independence makes it difficult to see much more than a family resemblance. We are scattered far and wide, and we are so completely given to our Father's business we really haven't had time lately to have a family portrait made.

As far as the power structures of our modern world are concerned, this band of brothers is not of much consequence. The world looks at us as insignificant and irrelevant—as it has always considered true Christianity—on the outskirts of the mainstream. From time to time, most of us wish one of us were called when the President needed someone to pray at his inauguration or when CNN wanted a religious counterpoint. *But that call doesn't come.* The call we have received is very different. Our power has never been about the White House or the Senate or the big company. The Kingdom we seek is not of this world. Our warfare is won in our own hearts, our conquests in the changed hearts and lives of people in our communities and in far-flung lands. Our victories are won one eternal life at a time.

As a group, we do not identify with the modern day protestant orthodoxy or the non-denominational evangelical movement. We don't typically show up in popular "church" polls and most secular studies because our association with one another is so loosely knit. And we can't point to a start date or founder—other than Christ.

So who are we? What are our values? How many of us are there? What are our churches like? What is going on in the fields where we serve? Are we healthy and growing or sickly and dying? Are we making the salt-and-light difference our Lord commanded us to make? If our nation or any other is ever to be blessed or preserved, it will be through the influence of a righteous minority. So are we a righteous minority or a saltless savor?

Describing the state of independent Baptist churches has been challenging. First of all, in the broader picture of religious movements, we are quite young. While our practices, principles, and forefathers trace back to the New Testament, most of us would say our modern roots, being called "independent Baptists," only go back sixty or seventy years. Second, we are doers of the Word, not researchers ensconced in the ivory towers of academia. Most of us would prefer to talk about what is happening in our own churches or in another church—but to actually study what happened and write it down is for the academics. It is not that we disdain those important endeavors, but who has time for such research when we are busy about the Father's business? For better or worse, we have been a largely undocumented group, at least in our present state.

It is precisely this lack of information that has compelled these authors to undertake this project. It is not because we have a fondness for statistics or a theoretical curiosity about the independent Baptist landscape, but because we have a passion for reaching precious souls for

Christ, and we have a commission to make disciples. Our conviction is that we need to know how we are doing. What we are doing *well* needs to be shared widely so others can learn and benefit from biblical practices. What we are *not* doing well needs to be known and corrected so we can be better stewards of the charge our Master has given us.

We hope that the following research will provide some perspective on who we are, where we came from, and where we must go in the days ahead.

WHERE DID WE COME FROM?

Through the ages, we identify with groups of believers who have elevated the clear teaching of Scripture above traditions, organizations, and denominations. These were the believers who fiercely fought for the autonomy of each local church and were persecuted for their belief in salvation through Christ alone, baptism after conversion, and other biblical convictions. Their detractors and persecutors through the centuries have unceasingly labeled them with various names and stigmas. They were martyred, imprisoned, persecuted, and reviled, but they continued steadfastly in the faith of Christ.

Our associations are loose, but our biblically-held convictions are distinct. It is our doctrine, our practice, and our local church philosophy that bring us together and reveal the family resemblance.

In the early twentieth century, a common outcry against the rise of German rationalism and humanism drew us to identify with a movement. This movement did not *define* us, but was supported by our kind because it stood for pure Bible doctrine in a day when several essential doctrines were under attack. Bible believers everywhere were alarmed and took seriously the admonition to "earnestly contend for the faith." This movement became known as *fundamentalism* and its supporters—fundamentalists. While the movement was protestant in origin and primarily led by para-church organizations, Bible-believing Baptists identified and supported the efforts to stand against liberal theology and harmful "-isms" such as Darwinism and rationalism. Fundamentalism began among conservative

Presbyterian theologians and soon spread to conservatives among many denominations and groups including Baptists.

The strength of this movement—fundamentalism—was that it upheld the core doctrines of God's Word which are essential to salvation (the virgin birth, the blood atonement, the deity of Christ, the inspiration of Scripture, and the bodily Resurrection). And the movement gave birth to Christian universities, para-church groups, and periodicals—all of which served to bring many people to Christ over many decades.

The flaws of this movement are two-fold: first, fundamentalism, by its nature and history, is improperly *inclusive*. Many pastors and leaders who might not have ordinarily had ecclesiastical fellowship due to significant doctrinal differences (such as infant baptism or eternal security) were united against a common enemy and for the common cause of defending the essentials of the faith. For instance, the founder of one fundamental institution, who formed his college as an interdenominational organization, said about matters such as eternal security, that where good men have differed, people should not make an issue over the divide.

Second, fundamentalism is by its nature improperly *exclusive*. Gradually, a certain segment of Bible believers came to think that these five fundamental doctrines and our willingness to stand for them were the sum total of our faith and the only test of purity and fellowship among God's people. The movement leaves out many vital Bible doctrines that Baptists would consider essential such as eternal security, the biblical mode of baptism, autonomy of the local church, the ministry of the Holy Spirit, and dozens of others.

As a movement, fundamentalism has faltered somewhat. Over the years, the para-church organizations (colleges, universities, ministries, and periodicals) that once defined and sustained the fundamental movement have become either soft in their stand or less significant in their influence.

Independent Baptists did not come from this movement, but we did identify with it and still do. We are not afraid to be called fundamentalists, but the term falls short in authentically defining who we are and where we came from. While the name "independent Baptist" is relatively new, Baptists with our biblical doctrine and practice existed long before fundamentalism.

And independent Baptists are bigger than fundamentalism in that our biblical doctrine cannot be contained within five bullet points, and our strength was never found in para-church organizations such as colleges and publications. We were never denominational in essence, and our kind exist regardless of the rise or fall of man-made movements or denominations with which we have identified.

Why is this important? Because many today refer to us as fundamentalists. While this term is accurate, it is also incomplete and insufficient. Yes, we hold to five fundamentals of Scripture, but our foundation and heritage are much broader.

WHAT ARE OUR VALUES?

There are two primary words used commonly to describe our happy band of brothers:

Independent
Baptist

There are many other adjectives we use to describe ourselves—*premillennial, soulwinning, separated, and Bible-believing.* We like labels. We like people to know what we are and where we stand. We put these descriptions on our brochures and signs. In fact, sign-making companies that charge by the letter love to see us coming! While it seems we regularly add to the label list, let's consider the big two characteristics of independent Baptist churches.

Independent

We are an independent lot, and we believe in the autonomy of the local church—that each local church should be self-governed and accountable directly to Jesus Christ (Matthew 18:15–17). We believe that Jesus, not a denomination, is the owner of the church. Acts 20:28 states, "Take heed therefore unto yourselves, and to all the flock, over the which the Holy

Ghost hath made you overseers, to feed the church of God, which he hath purchased with his own blood."

Most of our recent forefathers left Baptist denominations in the early twentieth century. They felt these denominations were starting to compromise and were no longer serving the best interests of the local churches that founded them. Instead of starting other denominations, they chose to remain "independent"—believing this to be more true to the biblical pattern of first-century churches.

So we are not a part of any formal denomination. Our movement does not have a world headquarters. Each local church is free to operate in whatever way it deems appropriate—recognizing a direct accountability to Christ. Some of us join *fellowships* (loose-knit groups of similar churches), but only for the purpose of having a group of like-minded churches with which to cooperate on matters of missions, education, and fellowship. We will not have the local church bound by any authority but the Lord's.

We are aware of the consequences of independence. For instance, we have no national voice. In the past, very few of our pastors have ever had a national constituency or were able to speak for us on a national level. Also, we are aware that independence can create *perceived* difficulties for overseas missionary outreach. We have no "cooperative program" among our churches to fund mission endeavors and retirements. It takes great personal effort and sacrifice for our missionaries to obtain the financing necessary for their work around the world.

Yet, we accept these *perceived* limitations because we believe that God blesses His work when done *His* way. We have weighed the alternatives of denominational influence and have seen the resulting decay. We believe that God will bless obedience to biblical patterns. Our choices in these matters have absolutely delivered a more acceptable and fruitful outcome.

For instance, if one or a few of our churches drift doctrinally or philosophically, the whole of us doesn't significantly suffer. But when denominational headquarters drift from their moorings, entire denominations and all of the associated institutions are impacted negatively as well—for generations to come. If one of our colleges begins to drift, soon enough growing churches will start another, and like-minded churches will support it. If one of our periodicals falters, soon enough local churches will start another, and similar churches will benefit from it. If a camp or other organization changes its position or direction, soon enough, our churches will start another to replace it.

We believe that God's Word is clear—the local church is the greatest and highest institution for God's work on earth. Our para-church organizations exist to support local churches and give account to them. It all begins and ends with the local church.

Thus we are independent by *conviction* and by *choice*.

Baptist

By far, our favorite term in defining ourselves is *Baptist*. Our "Baptist" doctrine is "Bible" doctrine—it originates in the pages of Scripture and not in the traditions of men. As a whole, we have resisted the modern trend of removing labels from our churches—to be fellowships, community churches, or non-descript groups of Christians-at-large. We want people to know precisely who we are, what we believe, and how we practice our faith.

For example, everyone is glad that the cans in grocery stores are labeled so we know what is in them. How hard it would be to shop at a store whose shelves were filled with unlabeled cans! You would have to take a can home and open it up to find out what was in it! And can you imagine restaurants taking off labels like *Mexican, Italian, or French?* We at least need a reference point to begin deciding whether or not a restaurant is acceptable to our taste preferences.

How much more important it is to define and label beliefs which flow from biblical conviction! How much more important it is to know the faith and doctrine of the church you attend. The *Baptist* label is important, and many have used it as an acronym to explain specifically what we believe. The following acronym provides a list of Bible doctrines that, to some degree, other denominations or groups do not hold:

Biblical authority—Our belief and practice comes from the Bible and not the traditions of men or church authorities (2 Timothy 3:16–17; 2 Peter 1:21).

Autonomy of the local church—Our churches are self-governing and give direct account to the authority of the Lord Jesus Christ (Colossians 1:18; 1 Timothy 3:15).

Priesthood of the believer—Every believer is accountable directly to Christ and has direct access to His throne through a personal relationship without the necessity of a human priest or mediator (1 Timothy 2:5–6; Hebrews 4:14–16).

Two ordinances—We believe in practicing the two ordinances that Jesus commanded—baptism and the Lord's Supper (Matthew 28:19–20; 1 Corinthians 11:23–26).

Individual soul responsibility—Every individual must come to Christ personally and make an individual choice regarding salvation and a relationship with Christ (Romans 10:13–17, 14:1–8, 12–23).

Saved, baptized church membership—Our local churches must be comprised of saved and baptized members as is patterned in the book of Acts (Acts 2:41).

Two offices in the church—Our churches are governed by two offices—pastors (synonymously referred to as elders and bishops in the Epistles) and deacons (Acts 6:1–7; 1 Timothy 3:1–13).

Separation of church and state—Our churches do not cooperate with a state-supported system of religion and must remain free from government control according to the biblical pattern (Matthew 22:21; Acts 5:29–31).

Often the acronym might include the **security of the believer**—our stand that the Scriptures teach eternal security (John 10:27–28; 1 Peter 1:3–5).

To some, the name *Baptist* is like a brand, and many think it is just another protestant denomination. To others, the name represents hundreds of years of suffering and struggle. Tens of thousands of men, women, and children through our history have given their lives because they refused to yield their beliefs in the face of tremendous persecution—specifically for what the name Baptist stood for in practice and doctrine.

In addition to the five fundamentals listed on page 8 and the above Baptist distinctives, the following doctrines are held as essential tests of fellowship by some independent Baptists and not by others:

Eschatology
Bible versions
Soulwinning
Church tradition
Personal separation
Dress standards
Musical styles
Ecclesiastical separation

As independent Baptists, we were originally much broader in our circle of fellowship when most Christians held to biblical lifestyles and practice. In recent decades, however, as doctrine has eroded in so many quarters, many among us have tightened the circle of fellowship.

Considering all this, one of the great things about being independent is that we can fellowship with whom we want as long as we are willing to accept the consequences. The only real outside control on us is the disdain or delight of other brothers. Some in our ranks have had an unapproachable spirit which has resulted in the tendency of others to make grievances public rather than handle them privately. Other public grievances have been borne more out of envy or ego than biblical principle.

But on a larger scale, we are accountable to Christ and to one another, and most of us greatly appreciate this accountability and benefit from iron-sharpening-iron relationships with our brothers. We don't have a problem confronting doctrinal shift or compromise among ourselves—although we could stand to grow in our approach and receptivity at times.

Future generations could greatly benefit from a compassionate, transparent kind of brotherly confrontation that could be received with a genuine spirit of humility and approachability. And we would be well served to choose our battles based upon Scripture and not personal preference. We could all benefit from a spirit that takes conflict or disagreement to a brother privately for resolution, rather than publishing it from the mountain tops. We will revisit this topic toward the end of the book.

While we adhere to our biblical principles, independent Baptists are experiencing a wonderful new paradigm in our leadership. The leadership of our movement is not coming from para-church organizations as in the past. Leadership is coming from the local church, and future leaders are being trained by local churches. What a blessing! The God-ordained, New Testament institution of local Baptist churches is now the place we send our young people for ministry training. These are the places where we gather for fellowship and encouragement. These are the places that provide models for biblical ministry philosophy. And so it should be!

For too long, para-church institutions have been seen as the conscience of those who hold to fundamental biblical doctrine, the voices of our position, and the institutions to which we look for help in responding to the issues of the day. While God has chosen to use and bless many such organizations over the years, there is no greater organization on earth to do God's work than the local church.

HOW MANY OF US ARE THERE IN THE U.S.?

Our research indicates we number 2,474,200. In 2005, there were 2,057,850 of us. So, over the past three years, we have grown by about 20%. That was a bigger number than we anticipated and very encouraging news! In a day when church attendance nationally is declining, what a joy it is to see this loose-knit group of local churches actually *growing* and reaching people for Christ!

Yet, the significance pales a bit when you look at the big picture. At this moment, there are an estimated 306,464,975 people in America.[1] About one out of every 125 people in America is an independent Baptist. That is about the same number as the population of the prison system in the United States or the population of Chicago.

So, while we rejoice in fruit, we certainly have some room to grow—and a great challenge before us.

HOW DO WE COMPARE IN SIZE TO OTHER GROUPS?

Independent Baptists are a collection of churches that share a similar set of core values, but how many churches are there? By sorting through a variety of mailing lists and sources, we were able to secure the names of 13,719 unique independent Baptist congregations in America. To put that into context, there are approximately 44,696 Southern Baptist churches. In terms of the country's population, for each independent Baptist church, there are nearly 22,300 lost Americans who need to be reached with the Gospel.

The following table also helps put our numbers into context.

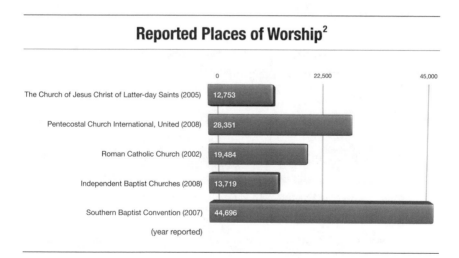

Reported Places of Worship[2]

	0	22,500	45,000
The Church of Jesus Christ of Latter-day Saints (2005)	12,753		
Pentecostal Church International, United (2008)	28,351		
Roman Catholic Church (2002)	19,484		
Independent Baptist Churches (2008)	13,719		
Southern Baptist Convention (2007)	44,696		
(year reported)			

WHAT SIZE ARE OUR CHURCHES?

According to our research, the *average* independent Baptist church has approximately 180 different people attending services sometime during the week. About 133 people in that church attend Sunday school. In 2005, the average independent Baptist church would have averaged about 150. So the average attendance in our fundamental churches has increased by about 30 people over the past three years. This is a tremendous and revealing statistic considering that nearly every other church group or denomination has seen attendance declines in the past three years. Of course, those numbers vary greatly based on a church's location and whether it has a bus ministry.

The *average* church size, however, may not be the most helpful number for understanding our congregations. In statistical terms, the average number is called the *mean*, and we all know you would arrive at average attendance by adding up all the attendance numbers and then dividing by the total number of congregations.

Another way of looking at our churches that may be more helpful is to describe the *typical* church. In statistical terms, the typical number is called the *median*. The median church attendance is the one in the middle of all the others—half the churches are bigger and half are smaller. The reason the typical (median) number can be more helpful than the average (mean) is that large discrepancies sometimes occur between the two. For example, the massive size of our largest churches pulls our average numbers upward to the point that they don't really represent the rank and file congregation. The "average church" is a statistical concept, but the "typical church" is a real congregation.

A *typical* Baptist church would have fewer people attending than the *average* of all independent Baptist churches taken together. Our research shows that a typical independent Baptist church has about 100 people in weekend worship and 70 people attending Sunday school. This paints a dramatically different picture of our congregations.

From these two numbers we can easily see that there are many strong independent Baptist churches, but also some weak ones. Not every independent Baptist church has seen an upward growth curve, and not all of them are experiencing the health and vibrance that many are. We do not define a strong church by its size alone, but rather by its health and growth. We will later explore the subject of *health*—whether a church is successfully reproducing disciples of Jesus Christ.

(At this point, we would encourage the reader not to begin drawing conclusions. It would be easy to start jumping to assumptions—either positive or negative—depending upon your perspective. As we share data in these early chapters, please refrain from passing judgment. We will spend the bulk of this book studying Scriptures, interpreting data, and drawing conclusions based upon this information. For now, please try not to interpret data as being either good or bad.)

Our research also identified some other key characteristics of independent Baptist churches:

Most of our attendees drive to their churches, but around 6,500 of our churches (less than half) have bus ministries, and about 280,000 people (mostly children) ride those buses to church. The average bus ministry involves about 44 children.

Geographic Regions

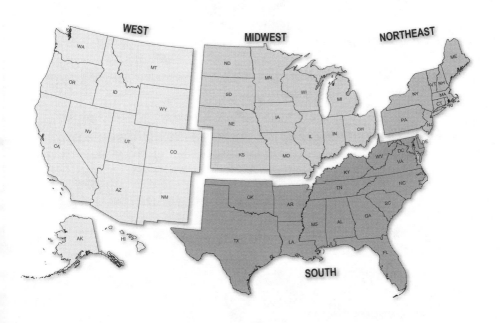

As the graphics below show, independent Baptists are much more likely to be located in the South or Midwest—leaving a lot of room for growth and expansion in many parts of the country.

Who are we, this band of brothers? Some of us wrestle with the fact that our churches are small and our national influence *seems* insignificant. Some see large churches on television and read about the influential churches in our past and wonder whether we are losing our relevance in and impact upon our society. Are these conclusions valid? If so, what

Number of Independent Baptist Churches by Region

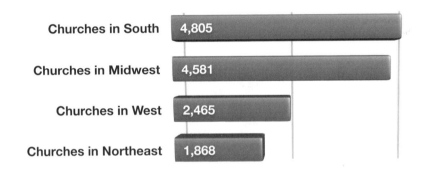

2008 Independent Baptist Church Worship Attendance

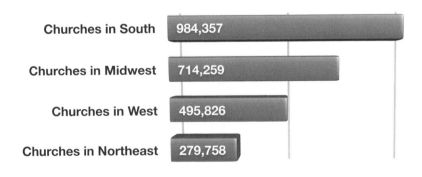

discouraging news! Consider this statement very carefully—much of this book hinges upon it:

Independent Baptists have never been a mega-church movement.

In fact, the local church since the time of Christ has never been a mega-church movement. That is not to say there were not mega-churches in the first century—for it would be hard to dismiss the church at Jerusalem which had thousands saved, baptized, and "added unto them." It is simply to say, mega-churches have never been the norm for the local church of Jesus Christ.

Some of our greatest leaders in the past were used of God to pastor mega-churches, but those congregations were far from the norm. Even in the '70s and '80s when we had some well-known larger churches, these were not representative of the bulk of us. Most of God's work through the centuries and in recent days has been accomplished through the significant influence of median-size local churches. Size does not determine influence—God's power and blessing does. As far as we know, the church at Antioch was not a "mega-church" but was responsible for sending the Apostle Paul and the Gospel into the known world.

We thank God for our independent Baptist mega-churches today. They provide resources and educational opportunities like colleges. They offer a place where large numbers of us can gather for fellowship or training. But mega-churches have never been the norm of this band of brothers.

The vast majority of us go to churches that average about 100 in attendance. These congregations and their pastors are the backbone of a very effective and fruitful movement of faithful local churches that has persisted since Jesus started the New Testament church.

The goal is not to become a mega-church movement. We want to reach every person with the Gospel, but the goal for your church should not be about size or numbers. The goal is to be the local church of Jesus Christ—to be what He desires and to do what He commands. If you are reading this book so that you might one day lead a mega-church, you have picked up the wrong book.

Do you feel constant pressure that your church must be bigger? Do you find yourself comparing church with church—yours always falling short in some way? Have you been tempted to look over the fence at the modern day "seeker-sensitive" movement that is attracting crowds in record numbers? Do you equate *size* with success or failure?

Perhaps now would be a good time to release some of that self-imposed pressure before reading further. The church is not a business or secular corporation, and its success cannot merely be measured in attendance charts and financial graphs.

If you pastor or participate in a small, independent Baptist church, you are a part of something very big in the eyes of God!

The rest of this book will challenge you and your church family to be a biblical church—and the Lord will determine its size. We challenge you to take your eyes off of numerical goals and focus rather on spiritual goals of soulwinning, discipleship, labor, service, and sincere ministry offered to Christ in obedience to biblical patterns. God will add to the church, if we will obey His Word.

Now we know more about what independent Baptists look like, but serious questions remain. Are our churches effective? Are we fulfilling the scriptural mandate of the church? Is God pleased with this loose-knit band of brothers? Are we really making a difference?

CHAPTER ONE
TAKE–AWAYS

- Independent Baptists are a band of brothers bound together by Christ and pure Bible doctrine.

- Our beliefs and practices trace to the first-century church.

- Our associations are loose, but our convictions are distinct.

- The term *fundamentalism* does not define us adequately.

- We are independent by biblical conviction.

- Baptist distinctives are biblical distinctives.

- Almost 2.5 million Americans are independent Baptists.

- There are over 13,700 independent Baptist churches in America.

- Our average church size is 180, but our typical church size is 100.

- Most of our churches are located in the South and Midwest.

- We have never been a mega-church movement.

VITAL SIGNS

"Remember therefore from whence thou art fallen, and repent, and do the first works; or else I will come unto thee quickly, and will remove thy candlestick out of his place, except thou repent."—Revelation 2:5

Why should we look at statistics to gauge the health and effectiveness of independent Baptists?

Suppose you wake up one morning with a bad stomachache. When you get to the doctor's office, the nurse has you fill out a form that lists illnesses you have had in the past and the medications you currently are taking. She asks you to step on the scale and records your weight. Then she asks you to roll up your sleeves and takes your blood pressure. You ask, "Why in the world do you need to know my height, weight, blood pressure, and current medications, when the problem is in my stomach?" Her reply: "The doctor needs your **vital signs** to begin his diagnosis."

Even if you felt fine and were only in the doctor's office for an annual physical, the doctor's staff would draw blood to analyze and put you on a treadmill to test your heart. Why? You feel fine! Because studying those test results could reveal a problem you aren't even aware of yet. Even if everything seems fine, climbing blood sugar or a slowly clogging artery guarantees serious problems ahead.

In many ways, some statistics are like vital signs. They do not always tell the whole story, but they help us understand the patient's health and can help us diagnose problems. Statistical vital signs even help us compare our overall health to others of similar age. During my (CR) last visit to the doctor, I saw a device on the waiting room wall that allowed you to enter your height and gender—then it gave an estimate of your ideal weight. While it couldn't be entirely accurate—your build and bone structure make a difference—for the most part, the machine gives a person helpful insight into whether or not they are at a healthy weight.

So how do you measure the effectiveness of our independent Baptist local churches? One indicator is our *vital signs.* As pulse and blood pressure are good indicators of the effectiveness of a person's heart, we identify key measurements that will indicate how well our churches are reflecting the heart of our God-given mission. The great mission given to the church is to take the Gospel to the entire world and make disciples. That is the heart of God's plan for our churches, and checking our vital signs will help us determine whether we as a group are "heart healthy."

The vital signs we measure must center on our mission. No one but God really knows the heart of our churches, but we can check our vital signs to see how we are doing.

The mission Jesus gave to the New Testament church is simple: "Go ye therefore, and teach all nations, baptizing them in the name of the Father, and of the Son, and of the Holy Ghost: Teaching them to observe all things whatsoever I have commanded you: and, lo, I am with you alway, even unto the end of the world. Amen" (Matthew 28:19–20).

GO EVERYWHERE AND MAKE DISCIPLES

So what do we measure to see if we are completing our mission?

One question we can ask is this: are we growing locally in our churches? Local growth is a natural byproduct of a church's healthy heart. The book of Acts makes it clear that when churches are healthy, people are being added to them. "Praising God, and having favour with all the people. And the Lord added to the church daily such as should be saved" (Acts 2:47). In Scripture, healthy churches grew.

So, are our churches growing? Our research reveals that, yes, independent Baptist churches in America are growing!

Independent Baptist Church Average Worship Attendance

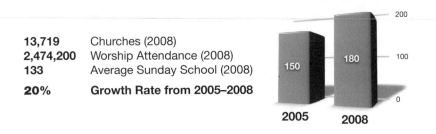

13,719	Churches (2008)
2,474,200	Worship Attendance (2008)
133	Average Sunday School (2008)
20%	**Growth Rate from 2005–2008**

When considering that similar denominations, such as Southern Baptists, are losing ground, we can be encouraged that many of our vital signs are at least on an upward trend.

Independent Baptist to Southern Baptist Comparison

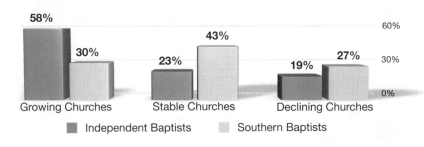

*(Current average worship attendance compared to fall 2005. Churches with growth of 10% or more are **Growing**; churches with a decrease of 10% or more are **Declining**; those in between are **Stable** or plateaued.)*

But local growth in and of itself is not the only indicator of church health. Church growth sometimes can be a little deceptive. Churches can grow even without people being saved and lives changed. Churches can grow by making unhealthy or unbiblical compromises in their programming—like those compromises of the "seeker-sensitive" movement. A congregation can grow larger by simply "adding fish from someone else's tank."

Another critical vital sign, therefore, is not only seeing numerical growth, but making disciples. This is the baseline of real ministry. Church growth is not healthy if it is accomplished without adding new converts and making new disciples. The real root of the Great Commission is making disciples. To get an idea of how we are doing in making disciples, we should ask the following questions:

Are people being saved?

Are converts getting baptized?

Are baptized converts becoming devoted Christians and long-term active members of our churches?

Question One—*Are people being saved?*

Yes, but at an alarmingly low rate. Our churches see one person saved per year for every 2.4 people attending our churches on Sunday morning (averaging 180 per worship service for 2008). Some churches were significantly higher and some significantly lower.

Average Saved/Baptized Per Year Per Independent Baptist Church

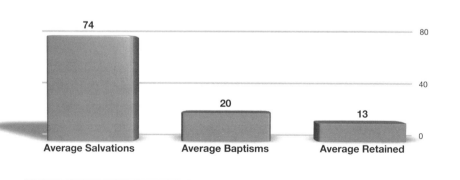

Percentages of Baptisms and Retention Per Year

Percentage of Baptized Converts

Percentage of Baptized Retained

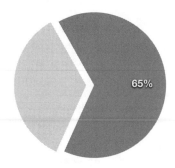

27%

65%

Question Two—Are converts being baptized?

As a whole, about only 27% of our converts get baptized. That means 73% of our converts never get to the first step of obedience to Christ. How can we be fulfilling the Great Commission if we never even fulfill the second element of the commission—"baptize"—with almost three-fourths of our converts?

Question Three—Are baptized converts becoming long-term active members of our churches?

About 18% of converts (65% of baptized) are being added to our churches as long-term active members. That means 82% of those who are saved never develop a long term relationship with our church. The Great Commission does not only tell us to baptize; it also commands us to teach converts "to observe all things whatsoever I have commanded you." While we would never under-value the importance of winning as many people as we possibly can to Jesus Christ—it is vital that we fulfill the entire Great Commission by seeing these new converts discipled through local church ministry.

These numbers hold pretty constant through many variations and subsets of churches. Some churches are baptizing and retaining a significantly higher percentage of their converts. Other churches see an incredible number of people saved, but a very small percentage baptized or discipled.

The Great Commission is only fulfilled when we complete the *entire* mission. The Great Commission is most powerful when it is completely fulfilled because then we see the *multiplication* of disciples instead of simply addition. Just as compound interest ultimately increases a bank account much more than simple interest, making disciples over the long term leads to far greater additions to God's family. The birthrate is slower at first, but the potential for multiplication is profound.

This disciple-making philosophy is clearly the teaching of God's Word in 2 Timothy 2:2 where Paul admonished Timothy: "And the things that thou hast heard of me among many witnesses, the same commit thou to faithful men, who shall be able to teach others also."

Another vital sign of church health is church planting. Church planting is a primary characteristic of New Testament Christianity throughout the book of Acts. As a movement, however, independent Baptists have seen a significant decrease in church planting activities over the past 15 to 20 years.

Number of Churches Started from before 1950–Present

New Churches Started Per Year

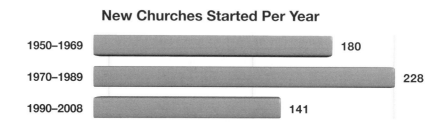

1950–1969	180
1970–1989	228
1990–2008	141

Total Number of New Churches Started

Before 1950	2,607
1950–1969	3,704
1970–1989	4,664
1990–2008	2,744

Total Worship Attendance of New Churches

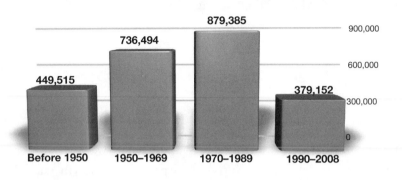

Using the start dates of the churches that completed our survey, we extrapolated the number of churches independent Baptists have planted in the United States over the past few decades.

Independent Baptists, of course, are not the only group seeing a decline in this area. All denominations and groups have seen an alarming decrease in church planting over the past decades.

Churches Started Per One Million Residents[1]

Based on start dates of 92,677 churches in the United States

As a whole, all of Bible Christianity is experiencing the lowest point of church planting in our nation's history. In *The American Church in Crisis,* researchers tell us that, "Every group with less than a one percent planting rate—less than one new church for every 100 established churches—is declining numerically in attendance."

For our independent Baptists to continue on the present course, we would need to plant 130 to 140 new churches each year, just to replace the number of churches we lose. According to our research, we are accomplishing that mission! On the other hand, the population of the United States is growing more rapidly than we are planting new congregations. For us to keep up with the population growth in the United States and improve our current situation, we would need to plant churches in a range of about 2% to 4% per year—about 275 to 550 congregations per year. We have significant room for improvement in this area.

Another vital sign is evangelizing the world outside the United States—Missions. When you look at finances, independent Baptist churches on average give about 19% of their income to foreign missions. Around 30% of the churches give 25% or more and, amazingly, about 19% of our local churches give 30% or more of their income to world missions.

Amount Given to Missions by Church Groups

Group	Number of Full Time Personnel Serving Overseas	Estimated Giving	Average Giving Per Church to Missions
Independent Baptists[2]	4,876 (1 missionary for every 2.8 churches) (13,719 churches)	$182,407,542	$13,295.98
Southern Baptist Convention[3]	3,898 (1 missionary for every 11.4 churches) (44,696 churches)	$197,866,000	$4,426.00
Assemblies of God[4]	1,199 (1 missionary for every 10.3 churches) (12,362 churches)	$177,262,833	$14,339.33

These statistics do not include independent Baptist *missionaries* and *money* sent directly out of churches without cooperation with clearing houses or mission boards. This is a large and growing number and would dramatically increase the numbers on the previous chart.

We are generously giving both our money and our people to take the Gospel around the world. That does not mean, however, that we are as effective as we could be in reaching the lost world outside of the United States with the Gospel. According to the 2008 Global Status of Evangelical Christianity, a staggering 3,907,986,328 people—that's 3.9 *billion* souls—in this world are completely unreached. Most of them have never once heard a clear presentation of the Gospel in a language they can truly understand.

If it were up to independent Baptists alone to evangelize the lost world, each of our missionaries would be responsible for reaching around 918,000 people with the Gospel. With the right strategy and teamwork, we could significantly lower this number in the coming years.

So what do our vital signs reveal? Our group is alive. Our heart is beating; we have a pulse. But some of our vital signs indicate problems that could lead to greater health risks unless we make some changes. Some of our churches seem to have a strong heart for the people who live around them, but they are weak in church-planting efforts. Some churches give huge percentages of their income and people resources to reach strangers, yet their local congregation is aging and their local outreach is ineffective.

And frankly, some of our churches are on life support. You can locate a pulse, but it is weak. That there is a pulse at all may have more to do with mechanical innovation and process than with authentic health. Promotional gimmicks and sensational programming may create the impression of healthy activity, perhaps even generating many public professions of faith—and we must be grateful to God for every precious soul that turns to Christ. But if few of those converts are ever baptized and even fewer are becoming long-term active church members, there is a problem. If our congregations are not planting new churches and multiplying disciples both at home and abroad, then our ministry activity is not as fruitful and the harvest not as plenteous as it should be.

Sometimes a person's health is directly related to his environment—external factors that can help or harm his vitality. Perhaps his home is infected with mold, or maybe he is severely allergic to contaminants in the air. Environment always plays a role in health.

By the same token, the evidence points to the fact that environmental factors also impact a church's health. Our study revealed several environmental factors that pose significant health risks among independent Baptist churches. We would do well to look at these "big picture" factors and respond wisely to them. We will see them in the next chapter.

CHAPTER TWO
TAKE–AWAYS

- In the past three years, independent Baptist churches have grown in attendance by an average of 20%.

- We are seeing an average of 74 people saved per year in our churches.

- Twenty-seven percent of our converts are being baptized.

- Eighteen percent of our converts are remaining faithful to church.

- Our church planting efforts have greatly decreased in the past twenty years.

- We need to plant about 500 churches per year to keep up with the population growth of our nation.

- Our churches give an average of 19% of our income to world missions. Many give more.

- Our vital signs reveal health in many areas, but also much room for growth and improvement.

THE FRUIT FACTORS

"Herein is my Father glorified, that ye bear much fruit;
so shall ye be my disciples."—JOHN 15:8

The Bible is rich with agricultural metaphors. In some ways, Scripture reads much like a Farmer's Almanac with long-range predictions. Agricultural lessons teach us about our lives as Christians—sowing and reaping and fruit bearing.

In the coming chapters, we will closely examine biblical practices that healthy churches employ to yield greater fruit. Where these practices were in place, we found health and strength in our research. Where they were lacking, we found weaker churches. But before we identify those practices, we want to examine a bigger picture perspective that came through in the survey.

As we studied churches across the independent Baptist landscape, we kept finding ourselves drawn to the metaphor of fruit bearing in regard to a large cross section of churches. We noticed that three key factors continually emerged which had a profound impact on local churches.

These three factors led to varying degrees of fruit bearing within our churches. They are as follows:

1. Fields (geography and environment)
2. Farmers (pastors and leadership)
3. Farms (type and age of the church)

Every farmer must understand his unique challenges in light of his field, himself, and his own farm. How well he adjusts and adapts to those challenges will greatly impact his harvest. For instance, if your field lacks a key nutrient, or if it's an old farm with specific soil challenges, you're just a smart farmer if you treat the soil and compensate for those deficiencies. If your ground requires a particular type of tractor or your age requires that you hire younger farm hands—you're just a better farmer if you address these challenges rather than ignore them.

We found that the more understanding one has of these three factors in local church ministry, the better one can produce the maximum yield on the plot of ground God has given to him—not by changing biblical principles or methods but by applying those principles and methods more strategically.

Be careful not to draw negative conclusions from what we are about to share. Let them make you aware of particular challenges you may face, and then respond wisely. These are important factors that impact your harvest, and it is wise to understand them. However, understanding them should encourage us to do our best in our God-given circumstances. In other words, these three factors must be understood and approached strategically in light of the local church harvest, but they should not be used to excuse a lack of health in local churches. Let us consider these areas more closely.

THE FIELD

Where is the church located? What part of the United States? Some states and regions of the country have been fertile ground for our independent Baptists up to this point.

Attendance and Growth Rate from Different Geographic Regions

	Number of Churches	2008 Worship Attendance	Avg. Sunday School	Avg. Worship 2008	Avg. Worship 2005	Growth Rate from 2005–2008
Churches in South	4,805	984,357	148	195	160	22%
Churches in Midwest	4,581	714,259	115	156	131	19%
Churches in West	2,465	495,826	147	199	172	16%
Churches in Northeast	1,868	279,758	99	150	130	15%

There are a higher number of independent Baptists in the South and Midwest. Churches in those areas experience a significantly higher growth rate as well.

The population of the areas where we find the majority of independent Baptist churches also is significant.

The vast majority of our churches are located in rural areas and small towns of less than 100,000 people. Our best growth rates are occurring in small cities and towns as well. Independent Baptist roots in the South and Midwest run deep. The West is a wide open door where new roots can be established. The Northeast is ripe for a rebirth and a replanting of the Gospel.

How Church Size Relates to Sizes of Cities and Towns

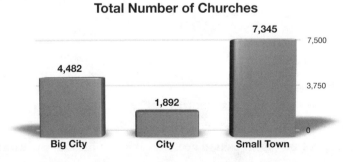

Total Number of Churches

How Church Size Relates to Sizes of Cities and Towns (cont.)

2008 Total Worship Attendance

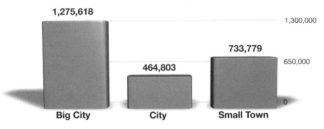

2008 Average Sunday School

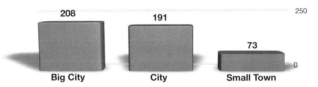

2005–2008 Worship Attendance Percent Growth

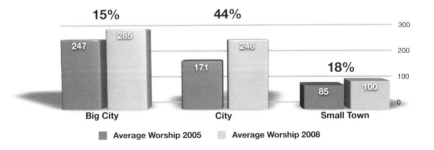

Jesus told a parable that contrasted the openness of some hearts to the Gospel with the hardness of other hearts. Matthew 13:23 says, "But he that received seed into the good ground is he that heareth the word, and understandeth it; which also beareth fruit, and bringeth forth, some an hundredfold, some sixty, some thirty." That does not mean we shouldn't plant churches everywhere, but we should be aware that some ground is more fertile for farming. Just as some individuals are more open to the Gospel than others, certain places have been more receptive than others. Understanding the relative openness of your area is crucial for discerning an effective strategy for evangelism and disciple-making.

THE FARMERS

Just as the productivity of a farm depends in part on who is farming it, another huge aspect of a congregation's "fruit factor" is the pastor himself. Consider the following trends:

Observations about farmers
Churches led by younger pastors grew at a faster rate.

Attendance and Growth Rate by Age of Pastors

	Number of Churches	Avg. Sunday School	Avg. Worship 2008	Avg. Worship 2005	Growth Rate from 2005–2008
Age of pastors 23–39	2,675	80	113	88	28%
Age of pastors 40–49	3,841	171	237	186	27%
Age of pastors 50–59	4,500	130	174	146	19%
Age of pastors 60+	2,703	143	185	170	9%

We must understand, of course, that smaller churches can experience a significant growth rate without adding a large number of people. A 10-member congregation that adds 10 more members experiences a 100% growth rate, while a 100-member church that adds 10 realizes only a 10% growth rate. In both size and percentage, however, the prime time for church growth is when pastors are between ages 40 and 49.

The fastest growth comes in the first two decades of a pastor's tenure at a church. That doesn't mean churches with pastors older than 40 or in their third decade of ministry can't lead growing or healthy churches—for there are churches and pastors that rise above the trends. Again, these are factors that we cannot ignore, but rather compensate for with strategic response. It certainly means we need our seasoned pastors to invest their knowledge, their hearts, and their lives more intentionally and strategically into younger pastors and in the efforts of church planting.

Attendance and Growth Rate by Tenure of Pastors

	Number of Churches	Avg. Sunday School	Avg. Worship 2008	Avg. Worship 2005	Growth Rate from 2005–2008
Tenure of pastor 5 years or less	3,951	79	109	80	36%
Tenure of pastor 6–10 years	3,251	97	139	118	18%
Tenure of pastor 11–20 years	3,800	143	196	166	18%
Tenure of pastor 20+ years	2,716	235	304	267	14%

Just as a successful farmer can, over time, enlarge his acreage, the largest churches are pastored by leaders who stay put. Over time, those congregations do not grow as fast, but they continue to grow. Steadfast and consistent leadership contributes greatly to local church health.

Two other interesting observations about farmers arise from the data. First, pastors with college degrees experienced a higher growth rate and a higher average attendance in their congregations. When it comes to farming effectiveness, there seems to be genuine value in being trained in conjunction with your calling. Of course, education is not everything. Some pastors who did not attend Bible college still experience incredible success. As a whole, however, there is a clear connection between pastoral training and congregational growth.

Attendance and Growth Rate by Education of Pastors

	Number of Churches	Avg. Sunday School	Avg. Worship 2008	Avg. Worship 2005	Growth Rate from 2005–2008
College degree	12,251	139	187	158	18%
No degree	1,468	62	87	76	14%

Second, as a whole, pastors who did not attend independent Baptist conferences actually *appeared* to grow at a higher rate than those who did. That is not the whole story, however. Not all conferences are equal. Many are geared primarily toward preaching and fellowship—which produce intangible results such as men deciding to stay faithful. Other conferences couple Bible preaching *with* training in ministry and church growth. We will refer to these as "equipping" conferences. Though the growth percentage number is lower, the pastors who attended equipping conferences actually added *more* people to their congregations than any other group, and their churches are larger as a whole (by an average of 46 people)—this explains the lower percentage.

Attendance and Growth Rate by Pastor's Training

	Number of Churches	Avg. Sunday School	Avg. Worship 2008	Avg. Worship 2005	Growth Rate from 2005–2008
Pastors attend conference	9,785	135	182	154	18%
Pastors do not attend conference	3,585	135	184	145	27%
Pastors attend Equipping conferences	2,266	180	230	187	23%

A small group of pastors attended both equipping conferences and other conferences.

So we see, when it comes to pastoral leadership—age, tenure, education, and ongoing training and fellowship all play critical roles in the health and long-term growth of a congregation. The trends we've seen, along with other key leadership metrics in the survey, confirm that effective pastoral leadership plays a huge role in bearing fruit. And effective pastoral leadership has much to do with three dynamics:

1. Developing a strategy to compensate for age and environment
2. Staying in one place for a long time
3. Continuing in personal education and training

OUR FARMS

The overall strength of a congregation also seems to depend on factors related to the church itself, especially the length of time the church has been in existence.

Attendance and Growth Rate by Church's Conception

	Number of Churches	Avg. Sunday School	Avg. Worship 2008	Avg. Worship 2005	Growth Rate from 2005–2008
Started before 1950	2,607	121	177	157	13%
Started between 1950–1969	3,704	159	204	174	17%
Started between 1970–1989	4,664	141	193	163	18%
Started between 1990–present	2,744	107	141	96	47%

Churches tend to be less productive over time. New churches register a much higher growth rate than older congregations. The findings in our study match a nationwide survey of churches of all denominations. Again, rather than draw concrete conclusions at this point, just be aware that these factors weigh significantly upon a church's fruitfulness and should be understood and considered carefully as we make ministry decisions.

The chart on the next page shows the growth trend of churches nationwide as they age. Younger churches tend to be where the most dynamic growth occurs.

These startling statistics speak powerfully to the necessity of church planting. All pastors should endeavor to have great growth locally—regardless of the age of your church, but these facts should compel us to

Yearly Growth Rate by Age of Church[1]

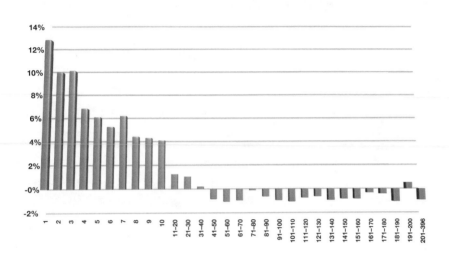

invest our efforts and resources into new and younger churches as well. They simply tend to produce more fruit. The best growth rates occur in our newest congregations.

Our sincere hope is that pastors will look at these statistics and realize that these three environmental factors—the fields, the farmers, and the farms—play an important role in fruit bearing. Noting these tendencies and factoring them into our leadership and outreach strategies can help us make wise decisions. This knowledge will help us be better farmers.

God, of course, can do anything anywhere. Paul said it like this: "I have planted, Apollos watered; but God gave the increase. So then neither is he that planteth any thing, neither he that watereth; but God that giveth the increase" (1 Corinthians 3:6–7).

Sometimes the Lord leads us to difficult places so only He will get the glory for what happens. He specializes in defying the trends and breaking out of statistical probabilities to do the impossible. We found great churches in our survey that sprang up in the most statistically unfriendly environments. For instance, God has raised up Lancaster Baptist Church in the most unpredictable place—a desert in California! We have studied great and healthy churches that defy the trends in each of these areas, and these churches say to us all, "God can!" "He turneth the wilderness into a standing water, and dry ground into watersprings" (Psalm 107:35).

But also, each of these churches sought to understand and respond wisely to the environment in which they ministered. They didn't throw out biblical methods such as preaching and soulwinning. Biblical principles are the same in every environment—they never change. Yet, as leaders, we must be aware of our environments and respond wisely that we might reap a greater harvest.

In addition to understanding the environment in which God has placed us, we also should be aware that wisdom is required to realize the best yield wherever we are serving. Once we have taken the field, farmer, and farm into account, we need to ask ourselves: which farming techniques will bring us the best yield?

CHAPTER THREE
TAKE–AWAYS

- Our local church harvests are directly impacted by three dynamics:

    Dynamic #1—geography, location, environment

    Dynamic #2—pastors and leadership

    Dynamic #3—type and age of the church

- These dynamics must be understood and strategically compensated for in each church.

- The West and Northeast are open doors for church planting.

- Churches usually grow faster in their younger years.

- Age, tenure, and education of the pastor are each significant factors in fruit-bearing.

- God can give us wisdom to respond properly to factors that could increase or decrease our harvest.

POSITIVE DEVIANCE

"And of some have compassion, making a difference:"
—JUDE 22

For 3,500 years, millions of people in West Asia and Sub-Saharan Africa have suffered horribly because of the Guinea worm. The Guinea worm is a parasite that is ingested as larvae when a person drinks stagnant and unfiltered water. The larva lodges in the stomach and grows into an enormous worm, sometimes as long as three feet! These worms excrete an acid that burns a path out of the body. People suffering from a Guinea worm will often ease the pain by dipping their limbs into ponds. The worm exits their body, then lays hundreds of thousands of eggs in the pond—and the cycle of destruction begins all over again.

Once a person contracts the disease, his life is drastically altered. He cannot farm, resulting in crop loss, which is followed by malnutrition and even starvation for his family. Children often must drop out of school to help take care of the family. Infections caused by the disease many times kill the victim. Generation after generation, families are affected. The Guinea worm is a huge barrier to progress.

In 1986, a research team from the Carter Center began to focus on the eradication of the Guinea worm disease. They found villages in Africa that should have suffered from Guinea worm disease but didn't. Even though these villages were drawing from the same water supply as people who lived in infected communities, residents of these villages were not infected.

As they studied the unaffected villages, researchers noticed the residents gathered water exactly as their neighbors did—with one difference. When the water arrived back in the village, the water was strained through a piece of cloth as it was poured into a second pot. The cloth—often the skirt of the woman carrying the water—would strain out the larvae and eliminate the majority of infections.

Armed with this knowledge, the Carter Center declared war on Guinea worm disease. In the ensuing years, an estimated 120 million people in 23,000 villages have been enormously helped by adopting this simple, but vital, preventive behavior.

Identifying key differences that solve problems is called "positive deviance." In the book *Influencer: The Power to Change Anything*, by Kerry Patterson, Joseph Grenny, David Maxfield, and Ron McMillan, positive deviance is described this way:

> "Positive deviance" can be extremely helpful in discovering the handful of vital behaviors that will help solve the problem you're attacking. That is, first dive into the center of the actual community, family, or organization you want to change. Second, discover and study settings where the targeted problem should exist but doesn't. Third, identify the unique behavior of the group that succeeds.

We implemented the concept of positive deviance in our research by segregating the 50 most fruitful and healthy churches with regard to growth and discipleship and compared them with the 50 least fruitful churches. We wanted to identify the traits of the strongest churches and draw out the "positive deviance"—identify what the stronger churches were doing that the weaker churches were not. This study was fascinating and challenging. Let's take a closer look.

THREE-YEAR PERCENT GROWTH/LOSS

The healthy churches we identified grew at an average rate of 9% a year, while the struggling churches shrank at an average rate of 6.5% a year. The fruitful churches saw a net growth of about 50 members per year, versus a loss of 13 per year in the weaker churches.

Three-Year Percent Growth/Loss

Three-Year Growth Rate

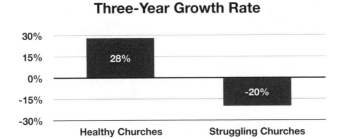

Average Amount of Growth/Loss

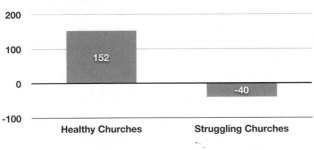

As we studied the traits among healthy churches, we discovered seven practices and principles that consistently proved to be "positive deviance." These are the qualities that were nearly always present in fruitful churches and absent in unfruitful churches. Not surprisingly, these are also qualities taught in Acts and in the New Testament Epistles. We will introduce them briefly here, and then more closely examine them one at a time in the next seven chapters.

SEVEN FACTORS OF POSITIVE DEVIANCE

The seven principles that healthy churches consistently practice are as follows:

1. Generate guests through effective outreach.
2. Create positive first impressions.
3. Connect God's Word with hearts.
4. Follow up biblically and strategically.
5. Use effective tools and technologies.
6. Compel spiritual commitments.
7. Develop devoted disciples.

1. Generate guests through effective outreach.

Strong churches believe in drawing people to their local church. They reach out to the community through soulwinning and visitation. They host events and Open Houses that welcome visitors, and they see themselves as ambassadors to their community. They work hard at bringing people to hear of Christ. Luke 14:23 says, "And the lord said unto the servant, Go out into the highways and hedges, and compel them to come in, that my house may be filled."

2. Create positive first impressions.

Strong churches give careful attention to their first impressions once their guests arrive. From their facilities to their greeters to the friendliness of the congregation—they realize you cannot beat the first impression. Nobody made a better first impression than Jesus—the multitudes just could not get enough of His compassion and power. Matthew 9:8 tells us, "But when the multitudes saw it, they marvelled, and glorified God, which had given such power unto men."

3.   Connect God's Word with hearts.

Strong churches minister differently to different age groups in the church (regardless of the size of that group), and they work hard at connecting God's Word practically to that age group. They see age-specific ministry and Bible-focused ministry as essential. As we observe the teaching and preaching of Jesus, it is apparent that He meant to be understood by the common man. He used stories, parables, and metaphors so He could connect the truth to their hearts. Scripture says in Mark 12:37, "…And the common people heard him gladly."

4.   Follow up biblically and strategically.

Strong churches know what happens to their visitors after the first visit. They have a clearly defined process of follow-up and reconnecting with those visitors personally. This process develops a relationship and ensures that the Gospel is shared and the next step of spiritual development is presented. Obviously this was the heart of the Apostle Paul in 1 Thessalonians 2:8, "So being affectionately desirous of you, we were willing to have imparted unto you, not the gospel of God only, but also our own souls, because ye were dear unto us."

5.   Use effective tools and technologies.

Strong churches see technologies as any other tool—much like a farmer would view a new tractor. Where they can employ tools or technologies to support any one of these practices without violating biblical principles, they do so—whether that be attendance and visitor tracking records, online websites, video projection, or any one of a thousand other ideas. They employ that which can enhance orderliness, efficiency, and communication, but they do not allow the *means* to overpower the *message*. Jesus used what was available and practical for ministry. Whether through story-telling, object lessons, or enhancing public address without electricity (such as speaking from a boat across a body of water), Jesus knew how to use the tools of His day to bring order to His ministry and strength to His message. Luke 5:3 says, "And he entered into one of the ships, which was Simon's, and prayed him that he would thrust out a little from the land. And he sat down, and taught the people out of the ship."

6. *Compel spiritual commitments.*

Strong churches are not afraid to compel people to take the next step in their faith journey—to teach people to obey God. They encourage them to take the steps that faith and growth require—to make biblical, spiritual commitments to Christ. Through preaching, teaching, and personal discipleship, they courageously create watershed moments when people must make choices about biblical commitments. Jesus did this throughout His earthly ministry. Luke 14:33 says, "So likewise, whosoever he be of you that forsaketh not all that he hath, he cannot be my disciple."

7. *Develop devoted disciples.*

Strong churches have a clearly defined process of personal discipleship in which they encourage new believers to participate in God's plan for spiritual maturity. They not only believe in 2 Timothy 2:2, but also have a strategy for developing relationships and authentic church life that makes this verse a reality. Second Timothy 2:2 instructs, "And the things that thou hast heard of me among many witnesses, the same commit thou to faithful men, who shall be able to teach others also."

These practices flow from biblical principles and are consistently present in healthy churches. Remember, they hold true across the survey—regardless of the subset of which an independent Baptist church is a part. In other words, these practices rise above the college name on the diploma, the conference one might attend, or the particular group with which a church most identifies.

Strong churches practice these seven points and have a goal of continually improving on them. Weak churches have lost them altogether.

Allow me (CR) to share a secular illustration of how the business or entertainment world has co-opted these biblical practices and applied them to their business model.

My family enjoys a vacation every year at the same resort. Because we have six young children, we used to have a difficult time finding suitable accommodations. During one of our recent visits, someone suggested we check out the timeshares. When we contacted the timeshare office, we were quickly coaxed into an incredible journey that transformed us from being "outsiders" to being fully committed timeshare owners!

How was it that we were so readily won over? Am I an easy mark for a slick salesman? No, this resort implemented these seven points of positive deviance that made the difference—and each point has a direct application to our study of strong or weak churches:

1. Generate guests through effective outreach. The timeshare planners are masters at generating traffic to the sales center. Kiosks were set up all over the resort, staffed by happy people eager to give you support and information, and to get you signed up for the timeshare tour. Brochures were left in our hotel room. Attractive signs everywhere espoused the virtues of joining the vacation club. The resort would actually arrange your transportation from anywhere on their property to visit their sales center.

2. Create positive first impressions. When we pulled up at the model timeshare, we were greeted by more happy people who seemed to be waiting just for us. The colors were theme appropriate, the grounds were immaculate, and the people were friendly. The view from the bus made us want to get out and go inside. The positive first impression was first class.

3. Connect God's Word with hearts. At the timeshare, each member of our family found something that was "thrilling" to them—connection! The staff showed the men the golf courses, exercise facilities, and restaurants. My wife was introduced to the spa and shopping areas. My children got a tour of the play areas and arcade. The staff knew how to engage the various needs of our family, and the timeshare went from being a cool thing we might do sometime in the future to a felt-need right now. Now, don't worry. We're not suggesting that we should put spas and golf courses on our local church campuses, and none of us has a resort-sized budget. We're merely pointing out how this company had every age in mind and connected their message with every person in my family.

4. **Follow up biblically and strategically.** We did not actually buy the timeshare the first time we visited. Was that the end? No. It was just the beginning. The resort had a carefully thought through long-term strategy of follow-up and relationship development. They wrote us letters, sent us reminders, emailed us, offered us discounts, and continually nurtured what began at the sales center. It was not pushy, but rather genuine and personal. They worked diligently to answer our questions and resolve our objections. Before we ever made the purchase, we felt as though we already had a relationship with the resort. Frankly, I don't think they would have ever dropped me off their list as a prospective owner unless I specifically asked them to. Now that's strategic follow-up.

5. **Use effective tools and technologies.** This resort skillfully leveraged every technology tool they could to more effectively and efficiently communicate with us—web, email, databases, video, audio, and creative presentations. They used these technologies in thoughtful ways. They did not rely on the technology to build the relationship, nor did the technology over-shadow the message. They simply used every "farm tool" at their disposal to cultivate a relationship with my family.

6. **Compel spiritual commitments.** The sales reps worked hard at getting us to capture their vision. Some visitors just showed up to collect the free gift they got for taking the tour, but the sales reps believed if you would give them a few moments of careful consideration, they could get you to see the benefits for yourself. They made a concerted effort to draw us into their family in a compelling and attractive way. They weren't afraid to nudge us into "the next step."

7. **Develop devoted disciples.** His name was Bill Koontz. Bill was not a high-pressure salesman with my personal bankruptcy in mind. He was someone who truly believed in the timeshare concept and believed he was helping my family. He seemed to feel that everyone could benefit from getting involved in this incredible concept. He was personally and

passionately connected to the vision, and he was not just selling a part-ownership. He was transferring his commitment to the vision. He not only wanted us to be owners, but fellow salesmen sharing the dream with others. And here I am—writing about it to complete strangers!

Again, I realize this is a secular illustration, but I could not get away from the commitment of the resort staff. I wondered this:

Have we, as leaders of independent Baptist churches ever thought through our outreach and discipleship processes with this kind of detail? Have we ever compelled someone to commit to Christ with the passion and delight with which Bill Koontz compelled me to buy a timeshare? Do we have any technology or structure that strategically supports how we develop relationships with searching hearts? Do we know where our guests end up after their first visit? Do we ever even see them again?

The timeshare sales people were enthusiastic, passionate, strategic, and focused on bringing you into their family. Think for a moment about how much more powerful, eternal, and wonderful the "product" we share! We have the answers to the world's most pressing problems. We are entrusted with introducing people to the Saviour of the world—the answer to their heart's deepest needs.

Have we thought it through, or are we "shooting from the hip"?

Independent Baptist churches that are reaching the world around them have adopted these positive deviance practices from Scripture, and they continuously strive to improve on them. Over the next seven chapters, we will examine each of these in greater detail and in light of God's Word.

1. Generate guests through effective outreach.
2. Create positive first impressions.
3. Connect God's Word with hearts.
4. Follow up biblically and strategically.
5. Use effective tools and technologies.
6. Compel spiritual commitments.
7. Develop devoted disciples.

CHAPTER FOUR
TAKE–AWAYS

- Our strongest churches grew in attendance by 28% in the past three years.

- Our weakest churches decreased in attendance by 20% in the past three years.

- Healthy churches consistently focus on seven biblical practices.

- Struggling churches have deviated from these same biblical practices.

- The seven biblical practices describe a process that helps a person journey from "first-time guest" to "devoted disciple."

    1. Generate guests through effective outreach.
    2. Create positive first impressions.
    3. Connect God's Word with hearts.
    4. Follow up biblically and strategically.
    5. Use effective tools and technologies.
    6. Compel spiritual commitments.
    7. Develop devoted disciples.

- We must think through our strategy both for reaching people and for developing them to spiritual maturity.

PART TWO

SEVEN PRACTICES OF HEALTHY CHURCHES

W e must make a critical distinction as we proceed. God is bigger than data and statistical probabilities. He tells us in Isaiah 55:8–9, "For my thoughts are not your thoughts, neither are your ways my ways, saith the Lord. For as the heavens are higher than the earth, so are my ways higher than your ways, and my thoughts than your thoughts." So often, His ways of blessing a church are beyond the realm of our strategies and planning.

Yet, at the same time, He intends for us to do the best we can with the information He provides to us. First Chronicles 12:32 tells us, "And of the children of Issachar, which were men that had understanding of the times, to know what Israel ought to do.…"

We must draw a distinct line between considering data and allowing data to set the agenda. The agenda is God's—the philosophy, the doctrine, and many of the methods have been clearly set forth in Scripture. These are not up for negotiation, reconsideration, or innovation. Again, our agenda is *duplication.*

And as we stated in the introduction, please be mindful that numerical growth does not always equal a healthy church. Regardless of its size, a healthy church can experience spiritual growth and have a profound influence.

In studying data and reliable research, we seek to gain an "understanding of the times." We do not seek to allow the times to dictate direction or principle. We seek to view data through the lens of Scripture that we might respond biblically and spiritually.

Where God's leading goes against statistical probabilities, go with God. Where trends may tempt you to distrust God's ways, reject the trends and go with God, "…for with God all things are possible" (Mark 10:27). Nothing is too hard for Him (Jeremiah 32:17).

The following chapters are delivered in the spirit and hope that we might bear much fruit (John 15:8).

In John 15:5, Jesus reminds us, "I am the vine, ye are the branches: He that abideth in me, and I in him, the same bringeth forth much fruit: for without me ye can do nothing." Apart from Him, our best strategies and plans will come to nothing. Without Him and His powerful touch, our understanding of trends and statistics will lead us down a dangerous path of constant reinvention and continual reconsideration of biblical principles. Let us not pursue or place hope in mathematical formulas but rather in Jesus Christ, for truly He is the center and source of all healthy, local church growth. For it is "God that giveth the increase" (1 Corinthians 3:7).

He has, however, entrusted to us the labor—the planting and the watering. In 1 Corinthians 3:6 Paul explained, "I have planted, Apollos watered; but God gave the increase."

The local church is not merely an organization, but an organism—a living entity—the body of Christ. Yet, we must take heed how we nurture and care for that body—how we build upon the foundation of Christ. First Corinthians 3:10 says, "According to the grace of God which is given unto me, as a wise masterbuilder, I have laid the foundation, and another buildeth thereon. But let every man take heed how he buildeth thereupon."

To that end we offer the following chapters—that we might "take heed" and be better farmers—that our sowing and nurturing efforts might be diligent, well-planned, strategic, and biblical.

Where God and human reasoning are in conflict—where statistics predict one probability and God's leading another—God's ways are true. Let the study give understanding, but let God determine your course. In this way, your local church will bear much fruit!

GENERATE GUESTS THROUGH EFFECTIVE OUTREACH

"And the lord said unto the servant, Go out into the
highways and hedges, and compel them to come in, that
my house may be filled."—LUKE 14:23

The Lord wants His house full. He has set His table with a great feast and thrown open the door. Some hungry people will walk by, see the "Free Banquet" sign, and come in. But other people are unaware of the feast. The banquet hall is not on the natural path of their everyday lives. So Jesus commands His servants to "compel" more guests to come.

Think about your church as a banquet hall where a great feast is ready to be served. Some people know your church is there because they live nearby or they drive by your location on a regular basis. (Do they know there is a feast inside?) But there are others whose daily paths take them in other directions. Do people in your town know your church exists? Are you making a compelling case for people to come in? Or is the light of the Gospel hidden under a bushel?

If our mission is to make disciples, we must bring potential disciples to our place of discipleship. Since the whole world is our prospect list, we have no want for potential disciples. It's getting people to church that facilitates the process of seeing them grow in their new faith.

The believers in Jerusalem were known for getting out the word about Jesus and their church. In Act 5:28, the enemies of the church testified about them: "…ye have filled Jerusalem with your doctrine…." Everybody in Jerusalem knew the church was there. They were effective at spreading the Word, reaching out, and bringing people to Christ.

A strong practice of healthy churches is consistent and effective outreach that continually labors to bring people to God's house. In this chapter we will refer to this as "guest traffic"—the continual presence of new faces in our services.

Does your community know that you are in their midst doing the Lord's work? Do they know that you are occupying till He comes (Luke 19:13)? Does everyone in your area have the regular opportunity to hear of Christ and be invited to your church? Healthy churches answer these questions with a resounding "yes!"

While the Bible mandates that our churches have open doors—open arms to the community—our outward message, often unintentionally, is "closed for business." This can be communicated through the appearance of the facilities, the condition of the church sign, the spirit of the pastor and people, or the regular level of outreach efforts. Many churches have an "us four and no more" mentality, and frankly their message is, "You are not welcome…."

For instance, what does your building and property say to the lost community around you—"Stay away" or "Come on in"? What about the spirit of the church family? When is the last time *you* experienced a typical Sunday at your church as a *first-time visitor*? Have you lived through that experience in your mind and heart?

Equally as important, how are you touching your community on a weekly and daily basis? Are you a constant visible presence of the Gospel or an occasional vapor? Are you touching every home in your community with the truth repeatedly or rarely—or never? Is there a good chance a first-time guest could discover your church, feel compelled to visit, find his way to your location, and feel welcome upon arrival?

Healthy churches practice biblical principles of reaching out and compelling people to come in to God's house—and they make that house as welcoming and inviting as possible.

When it comes to filling the Lord's house, consider two kinds of guest traffic:

Natural traffic—people who drive by the house and come in without an invitation.

Generated traffic—people who are "compelled" by the Lord's servants to come to the house.

NATURAL TRAFFIC

Every church location will generate some amount of "drive-by" or natural guest traffic. These are the people that come to your church through the providence of God—perhaps they saw your sign, drove by your building, or looked you up in some way. Some churches receive a significant amount of natural traffic because of the community's growth patterns or the church's location on a major highway.

The early church at Jerusalem met in houses, but they also gathered at the "temple." Acts 2:46 says, "And they, continuing daily with one accord in the temple, and breaking bread from house to house, did eat their meat with gladness and singleness of heart." The believers chose a well-known location that had "high traffic." They were determined to make an impact at the heart of their city.

By the same token, churches today that are located in declining areas typically grow at a significantly slower rate than churches in stable or escalating areas. Location does matter on a practical level:

Average Yearly Growth in non-declining areas: 6%
Average Yearly Growth in declining areas: 3%

A church fifty years ago may have been located in a growing area with great potential for drive-by traffic, but communities change, and over the years an area can become a backwater. Perhaps an ethnic transition has occurred and the people who now live around the church do not speak fluent English, but the church's program has not changed to meet the needs of its changing neighborhood. The people who do attend are no longer the residents' neighbors but drive to church from farther and farther away.

Most churches cannot relocate easily. Therefore, if God has put your church in a particular community—embrace that community with the love of Christ. The people who live around your church should be the first ones who hear and know of it simply because of this principle of natural traffic.

A farmer who knows his vocation will realize that his soil or location may require additional intervention to produce a good harvest, but that doesn't always mean he moves the farm. Instead, a wise farmer carefully adjusts his farming strategy to produce the maximum yield. He may use a certain kind of fertilizer or chemical nutrient. Perhaps he irrigates the land or uses a herbicide to control pests. In the same way, if a pastor knows his church has obstacles to natural traffic, he can determine what creative effort needs to be expended to generate more guests to the church.

Where you are matters greatly, but *how often* you tell people where you are matters even more—and both are completely trumped by an anointed preacher, because where there is an anointed man of God preaching the truth, people will come to hear it. Jesus is the greatest example of this. No matter where He was, multitudes showed up whenever possible.

Every church would love a great location, but most have to do the best they can with something less than ideal—and still others are needfully planted in rural areas where populations are sparse but still lost. Having a less than ideal location simply means you have to tell people where you are—longer, louder, and more often. Your outreach ministry must be more consistent and pervasive—inviting people to visit and to hear the truth.

Natural traffic is primarily about location and facilities. While we don't always have control over location, we do have control over the appearance and condition of our facilities. In this, we challenge you to have a standard of excellence.

Strive for excellence in your facilities. Mediocrity breeds indifference, but quality attracts. We must strengthen our efforts in maintaining our facilities so that people know we care about what happens in those buildings. This isn't about having the newest or the most expensive—it's about doing our best with whatever God has provided.

One of the first things that I (pwc) did at Lancaster Baptist was begin to make a broken down old building look as fresh, clean, and presentable as possible. I often say, "The first thing I did when I arrived in Lancaster was mow the parking lot." People always laugh because they think I'm joking—but it's no joke—I literally did mow the parking lot! We didn't have much money or much to work with in those days, but we did the best we could with what God provided. We painted, ripped up old carpet, replaced the sign, and freshened up dark and cluttered rooms. I believe God gave us better buildings because we took good care of the little that He gave us to begin with.

It's amazing what green grass, flowers, fresh paint, a colorful banner, and some balloons can do for an old building. These are not expensive things, but they say to passers-by, "You are invited and welcome to this happy place!" They provide an indicator that you value what happens in your facilities. A well-prepared place is inviting to outsiders.

When it comes to our commission, however, we were never taught in Scripture to rely only on natural traffic. We are commanded to go out and compel them to come in. The biblical pattern is that we should minister "daily and from house to house" (Acts 2:46, 20:20). This is where all of our outreach ministries and efforts apply—and for this chapter, we will call this "generated traffic."

GENERATED TRAFFIC

What drives more guests to a church location? We want to focus on two factors:

1. **The people**—*the spirit, words, and actions of your church family*
2. **The projection**—*the outreach, media, and materials you publish*

These two ideas are not mutually exclusive, of course. In fact, they complement each other. The more effectively you project your ministry into the community through quality media and materials, the more comfortable people feel when they are personally invited by the people within your church family. Let's examine these more closely.

The people

The most powerful tool in generating traffic to your church is an empowered group of people who are excitedly out in the community, talking about Jesus and your church.

Our survey asked pastors whether they agreed with the statement, "Our church is a soulwinning church." We found that members of healthy, growing churches were much more likely to be talking about Jesus in the community and seeing lost people saved. Consider the following statistics.

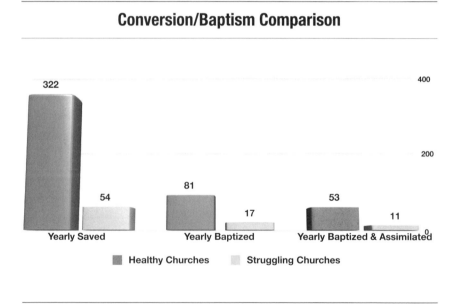

Conversion/Baptism Comparison

Knowing that conversion and baptism doesn't tell the entire story, we also compared the retention rates of healthy churches and struggling churches.

Retention Comparison

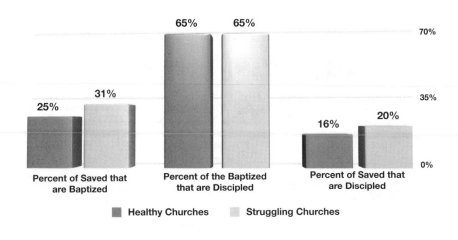

We were surprised to find that the retention of converts was not the big factor in the growth of churches. In fact, struggling churches are *statistically* better in retaining converts—but that's not the whole story because in these churches there are far fewer people to "retain," and often they are relatives and family members. The big factor was the *raw number* of converts. In other words, stronger churches generated higher traffic. The point is, declining churches are not risk-taking—they generally are not reaching out aggressively and seeing a lot of guest traffic and salvations. They are reaching fewer people, therefore losing fewer as well.

We also found that struggling churches were much more likely to agree with the statement, "Most of the conversions in our church are among children." We are not implying that the salvation of children is unimportant—thank God for every precious soul who comes to Christ! We are simply noting that healthy churches are reaching the people who decide where the family attends church. Little children are much more likely to come to Christ than adults. Jesus said, "Suffer the little children to come unto me, and forbid them not: for of such is the kingdom of God" (Mark 10:14). But Jesus also said, "Follow me, and I will make you fishers of men" (Matthew 4:19). In other words, while children are more likely to be natural traffic (brought to church by parents), adults must be fished out—generated traffic.

How do healthy churches develop an effective outreach? Based on our research, we identified four factors:

1. THE PERSONAL EXAMPLE OF THE PASTOR AND STAFF

Is the pastor the lead soulwinner of the congregation, intentionally seeking out prospects and leading them to Christ and your church? Healthy churches have soulwinning pastors—men whose spirits stir them to lead by example. Your church will reflect the pastor's heart for soulwinning and outreach. The pastors are the first mentors and models in ministry. For the outreach of a church to be substantive, the pastor and staff must be out soulwinning, bringing visitors to church, and being publicly accountable and fruitful in personal outreach.

Along these lines, healthy churches were much more likely to *require* their leadership to participate in soulwinning and visitation. Admittedly, we ought not have to "require" this sort of baseline, biblical Christianity—for it's already a command. But human nature being what it is, without these "requirements" this is often the first ministry to slip and suffer in the weekly schedule.

Francis Bacon, Sr. said, "He that gives good advice, builds with one hand; he that gives good counsel and example, builds with both; but he that gives good admonition and bad example, builds with one hand and pulls down with the other."

2. MEMBERS ARE EDUCATED AND TRAINED IN COMPASSIONATE OUTREACH.

Healthy churches are almost twice as likely to have structured evangelism training classes (7 in 10 versus 4 in 10 in struggling churches).

How do you equip the saints for the work of outreach? Healthy churches labor to invest the time, the resources, and the training that the church family might be good ambassadors for the Lord Jesus (2 Corinthians 5:20).

We must strive for excellence in personal and compassionate outreach. More than the classroom training of how to invite people or share the Gospel, the people of the church must be trained in how to *care* for people. This should mirror the compassion of the father in Luke 15:20 where the Bible says, "And he arose, and came to his father. But when he was yet a great way off, his father saw him, and had compassion, and ran, and fell on his neck, and kissed him." In 1 Thessalonians 2, the Apostle Paul details his heart of compassion—imparting his own soul unto the people because they were "…dear unto us" (v. 8). He speaks of cherishing them gently, "…as a nurse cherisheth her children" (v. 7).

In the same way, every church family should have open arms of love and compassion to every soul. The church family shouldn't be judgmental or harsh towards lost visitors who have never been trained and discipled in biblical living. We should lovingly accept the lost.

Independent Baptist churches have historically emphasized personal separation from the world. Thank God for this biblical emphasis. In some churches, however, personal separation is such an obsession that the spirit toward the lost is less than compassionate. The harsh environment and lack of patience inhibits the lost from coming to Christ and growing in His grace.

While there will be aspects of a lost person's life or lifestyle that we should not accept—we should accept the person in the love of Christ. While we cannot accept sinful lifestyles, we must have an accepting heart toward lost people. Jesus exemplified this in Matthew 11:18–19, "For John came neither eating nor drinking, and they say, He hath a devil. The Son of man came eating and drinking, and they say, Behold a man gluttonous, and a winebibber, a friend of publicans and sinners. But wisdom is justified of her children." Jesus was the friend of sinners, and because of this He reached sinners.

In this light, every relationship in a Christian's life should be leveraged to bring people to Jesus Christ, and your church family should be taught this biblical perspective. They should be taught how to reach out to the lost with Christ-like love.

When is the last time you opened your home for a meal or had a meaningful conversation with a lost person? How do you meet and connect with lost people in your community? Some pastors play basketball at a YMCA, others develop connections with city leaders or building project personnel. There are many ways to meet lost people, and we will not reach them if we don't first get to know them. Of course, Jesus was criticized by the Pharisees for eating with publicans and sinners (Matthew 9:11).

In a culture that is increasingly more hostile and wicked, we cannot afford to go into hiding. We are commanded to be salt and light, and our church families should be trained in being compassionate and soul-conscious even as they are taught holiness.

3. MEMBERS ARE GIVEN STRUCTURED OPPORTUNITIES FOR EVANGELISM.

Healthy churches are twice as likely to have scheduled door-to-door soulwinning times. Ninety percent of strong churches have regular times of outreach while only 50% of struggling churches do.

We are pleased to report that 70% of independent Baptist churches still go door-to-door soulwinning in their cities. We are aware that our critics have deemed this biblical method as impractical or ineffective. But, this practice is not only biblical, it is practical and effective. After all, if politicians will do it, why not Bible-believing Christians? The Scripture clearly teaches "house to house" (Acts 20:20).

This is the principle of *saturation*. Healthy, growing churches are consistently going everywhere in their community with the Gospel of Christ. We are to constantly, systematically, and publicly present Christ to our city. There shouldn't be a week or a season when we are not going out with the Gospel.

For example, Lancaster Baptist Church maps the entire Antelope Valley, which includes Lancaster and surrounding cities, and systematically works through every community and every street—taking the Gospel to every door. The soulwinning teams take maps, and they know exactly which streets to visit. They even know which doors to pass if someone in the neighborhood has specifically requested that the church not knock on their door. When they are finished, they turn the map in, notating which streets were completed. This is orderly and systematic—so as not to overlap or overlook an area. It requires planning and accountability.

It requires strategy and forethought. Every home in the valley is visited several times each year.

4. FREQUENT ENCOURAGEMENT FOR OUTREACH FROM THE PULPIT

Pastors of healthy churches were much more likely to agree with the following statements: "I often take the opportunity in my sermons to encourage attendees to invite others to attend church activities with them." "I often take the opportunity in my sermons to encourage believers to build relationships with non-believers to create opportunities to share the Gospel with them."

Preaching makes a difference. It compels people to obey the Bible—to trust God and follow His commands. This is the final piece of the puzzle. Once you are setting the example, providing training, and scheduling outreach—it is the preaching of the Word of God that will bring the conviction necessary for people to become involved in sharing Christ.

We see four strategies that God blesses—practices that consistently prove effective in growing churches—pastoral staff and leadership setting the soulwinning example, training the church family in soulwinning, providing outreach opportunities for soulwinning, and preaching biblical messages to encourage soulwinning.

Part of our research included asking pastors what outreach methods they found most effective in generating guests to their church. **A huge majority said the most effective way to identify prospects and get people to actually visit is a *personal invitation from someone they know.***

Without a doubt, the most effective way to generate guests is by having a spiritually motivated group of Christians—a whole congregation of Spirit-filled ambassadors—trying to get people into the Lord's house.

The effectiveness of these biblical behaviors was also borne out in a survey done many years ago by the Institute for American Church Growth, which asked 10,000 people about their pilgrimage to salvation and church membership. What led them into those relationships? Answers were as follows in the chart on the next page.

What Brought People to Church[1]

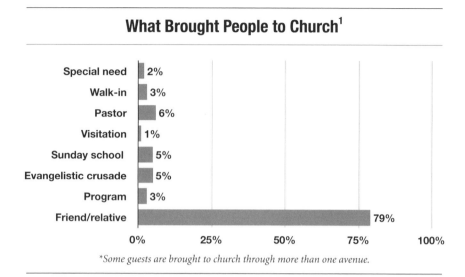

Special need	2%
Walk-in	3%
Pastor	6%
Visitation	1%
Sunday school	5%
Evangelistic crusade	5%
Program	3%
Friend/relative	79%

0%　　25%　　50%　　75%　　100%

Some guests are brought to church through more than one avenue.

There are, however, other factors that improve the effectiveness of your church family as they reach out into the community—factors that *project* the church into the awareness of community residents. For the farmer, these factors could be compared to plowing up the soil in preparation for the sowing of the seed. While your church members should be busy sowing the seed, there are some effective things you can do to prepare the soil for their labor. Let's take a closer look.

THE PROJECTION

Our research confirmed that healthy churches were much more likely to generate traffic by employing a variety of media, technologies, and programs to project their ministry into the local community. In Matthew 5:16 Jesus says, "Let your light so shine before men, that they may see your good works, and glorify your Father which is in heaven." We are to shine into our communities like a lighthouse so that, when we have their attention, people will see our good works.

Other than your facilities and your church members, there are hundreds of ways to project your church into your community, but a few are absolutely vital—in our research, they stand out as essential rather than optional.

SPOTLIGHTING CHURCHES THAT WORK

SOUTHERN HILLS BAPTIST CHURCH

SOUTHWEST LAS VEGAS, NEVADA

Southern Hills Baptist Church planted by Pastor Josh Teis is a third-generation church plant in Las Vegas. The church began August 1, 2004, as a church plant of the Liberty Baptist Church (a thirty-year-old church plant) led by Josh's father, Dave Teis. The church is now averaging over 300 after just four and a half years of ministry.

The Teis's began as staff members of Liberty Baptist, laboring in an extension work with twenty other Liberty members who helped them begin. They were also partially supported by other churches. Four months later the new church was officially chartered with 83 members, and Josh became the full-time pastor.

Josh shared six primary ways that first-time guests arrived at their doors.

"*Door-knocking is #1,*" he stated, "first because it is the *least expensive*. You just grab brochures and go." But that's not the whole story—for not all "door-knocking" is equal. When asked about his approach he focused on several critical thoughts. "Well, in the early days, my wife and I would knock on 100 doors per day together. People responded better when we went as a couple.

"I don't knock on doors in the morning, because many people in our area work the swing shift and are asleep. So in the morning, I canvass and leave materials on doors. In the afternoon, I'm knocking on doors to meet people, share the Gospel, and find prospects—but never with an overwhelming approach. Though we sometimes lead people to Christ at the door, far more people are saved after they visit the church—and usually these are the ones that stay faithful."

Describing *where* he knocks doors he said, "It really takes four or five times to the same doors before people even know who you are. I would rather go six times to the same zip code than door knock in six different zip codes. We door knock our closer zip codes four to six times each year. You must get out there and meet people. Nobody

SOUTHERN HILLS BAPTIST CONTINUED...

knows you're there, and nobody *cares* until you get out there and meet them!"

Nice brochures are vital. "We printed high quality, colorful brochures with clear directions. That made a big difference."

Signage. Josh used directional signs around the church to draw people, but he also thought creatively and "out of the box." "I bought 100 2'x2' plastic signs with our church name, start date, and phone number. We placed those signs along roads and anywhere we could get away with." The inexpensive signs generated a lot of phone calls to a new number that rang to their home. Josh said, "That worked really well. Even while out door-knocking people often said, 'Oh, I've seen your signs.' The positive far outweighed the negative, and there is some negative response, no matter what you do."

Mailers. "These are very expensive but we did what we could afford, and they did generate some response."

Neighbor day, coworker day, family day! "Everybody has them, so we hosted three different days and encouraged our church family to invite neighbors, coworkers, and relatives."

New move-in labels. "We contacted a company that provided names and addresses of people who moved into our community. Then we delivered a basket of cookies on what we called 'welcome to the neighborhood' visits. We encouraged our church members to visit 'that door and four more!'—to talk to the new move-in and then to knock on four more doors near that door. Several families have joined our church from this, and we still do it every week."

Since the first week, Josh has hosted Tuesday and Saturday soulwinning. "At first people didn't always come, but now there are always people at soulwinning. Just start having all-church soulwinning—and keep having it. Somebody's going to show up eventually. And when they lead someone to Christ, they will start coming all the time."

God is blessing the fantastic spirit of this young pastor and his passionate, creative strategy for bringing first-time guests to his church.

The church sign

The single most important tool for projecting your church into the community is perhaps the one most taken for granted. The church sign is a monster for generating traffic. Don't skimp on the sign!

The U.S. Small Business Administration makes the following observations about signs: A sign that is easily detected and read, no matter the time or weather, will pay for itself many times over during the course of your organization.

Signs are the most affordable means of advertising for many organizations, and most organizations—new or not—don't have a dollar to waste. What's more, signs are always on the job for you, advertising 24 hours a day, 365 days a year.[2]

Customers at Quick Service Food (QSF) restaurants were asked how they first became aware of the restaurant. The chart below tells the story:

What Brought People to Restaurants[3]

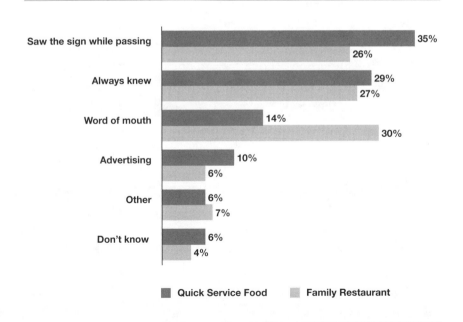

Successful organizations know the value of signage. Thomas James, a signage expert, notes: "McDonalds spends around $100K on signage (per location) to sell a 99-cent hamburger…Yet, the manufactured home dealer with great highway visibility puts up a $300 sign (selling a $75,000 hamburger) and then complains about low customer traffic." Don't underestimate the power of signage.

The church website

Another tool that has become enormously valuable in projecting a church into its community is a website. Richard Reising, president of Artistry Marketing Concepts, says as many as 85% of people looking for a church are finding the church by searching for websites. Reising says, "Websites are replacing the Yellow Pages as a key mode of church advertising."[4]

For most people today, a church's website is the new "front-door" and "lobby" of the church. Most people will "check your church out" online before they will ever actually visit your facility. Independent Baptists have been very slow in recognizing this trend and are missing out on a strategic opportunity to project themselves into the surrounding community—and even around the world.

In our study, we found that 9 in 10 healthy churches used the internet to build awareness of their churches. When we surveyed the websites of many healthy churches, we found that the sites were well designed, well maintained, and had strong content. Not all websites are created equal, however. Some of the sites we saw were underdeveloped and did not serve to attract a guest to the church. We would encourage you to put as much time and effort into the virtual front door and lobby of your church as you would invest in the physical entrance to your facility.

A website is much more useful when people know it exists. The following four ideas will help any church drive traffic to their website.

Have a memorable website address. You might find it easy to remember www.tx.rr.abc.friendlybaptist.yahoo.com, but the outside world will have a much easier time with www.lancasterbaptist.org.

Put your website address on *everything*. Your website address needs to be on your tracts, business cards, brochures, stationery, and ads.

It also should be prominently visible outside your location—perhaps as a prominent feature of your sign!

Start a monthly email newsletter. Give guests and prospects an opportunity to sign up for an email newsletter that provides periodic updates on your activities and ministries.

Get listed on map services. Google will list your church on Google Maps for free. When people use Google to look up a nearby address, your church will be shown on the map (link: http://www.google.com/local/add).

Excellence in printed materials

Next to your sign and website, the most powerful image you project to your community will be in printed form. Colorful, well thought-out print materials are the language of our culture—and we often fail to speak that language. For instance, why should Domino's Pizza have more attractive brochures than our local churches? Shouldn't we care more about souls than Domino's cares about selling pizza?

Your image in print defines your image to your community. If you don't carefully define that image, someone else will. Therefore, *we should strive for excellence in all of our print materials.* Work with a competent designer and adequate print facility to produce materials that are attractive, creative, well-worded, inviting, and memorable. The goal is to get noticed— to capture the attention of your community.

Place a small map on all church materials—tracts, flyers, websites, etc. Do everything you can to let people know you are in town and where you are in town. If you have an attractive photo of your building, use it in your print and web materials so your guests will know and recognize their destination. (For brochure and tract samples, visit strivingtogether.com.)

Other methods of "generating guests"

Our research also identified that healthy churches regularly use a variety of media, mailings, and other forms of projection to reach their community. These may include:

Servant evangelism projects
Mass mailings
Radio and TV ads/programs
Community newsletters
Public service announcements

The keys are quality, variety, and consistency. Churches that saturate their community seek to become a lasting presence. They advertise consistently, not sporadically. They establish a variety of ways to consistently be seen and heard by their area—and they vary the approach from season to season. They might use billboards for a while and then do direct mailings. Later they might run television or radio ads.

This isn't always about budget as much as priority. If generating guests through outreach is a priority, then projection will be a priority. You will determine to let your community know that your church exists, and you will consistently budget toward that end.

Finally, don't forget, all of the printed materials and media combined don't directly generate guests as much as they prepare the soil for the personal invitations of your church family.

I (PWC) remember a vivid example of how media can prepare the soil of hearts. Each year our church hosts an Open House when we invite the community to a special Sunday morning service followed by a luncheon. This particular year, we were running thirty-second television spots with me standing in front of the church inviting the community to Open House Sunday.

That week, while I was out door-knocking, a gentleman answered the door and dropped his jaw. As I stood there inviting him to church, he looked shocked. He then said, "I just saw you on TV not five seconds ago!" Needless to say, we had a great conversation; the media had paved the way for an open door.

Churches are more effective when they focus intentionally on the two ways that guests arrive at their campus—*natural traffic* and *generated traffic*. Realizing that God wants us to be a light on a hill (Matthew 5:14–16) should help us understand that our location and our projection are both important. When possible, choose a location with maximum impact—one that will receive the most possible natural traffic.

Of course, location, is not everything. Sometimes a good location and a growing area can create a level of natural traffic that masks a deficiency in generating traffic. A church might grow in spite of the fact that its people are not doing a good job of engaging their community, but that growth won't be as sustained and strong as it could be. Pastors must make sure they are setting an example and encouraging their members to compel people to come and fill up the Master's table. There is still room!

But what happens when the guests arrive? Is there a banquet feast prepared that honors the Lord and makes our guests feel welcomed and loved? That is the way the Master would have it, so let's move on.

CHAPTER FIVE
TAKE–AWAYS

- God desires for us to bear much fruit—He wants His house full.

- Healthy churches draw people to visit their church.

- Natural traffic is primarily about location and facilities.

- Generated traffic is primarily about outreach.

- Generated traffic happens through the people of the church and the projection (media and outreach) of the church.

- Healthy churches have pastors who lead by example in soulwinning.

- Healthy churches educate their church family in how to reach out to others.

- Healthy churches give the church family opportunities for evangelism.

- Healthy churches hear preaching about outreach.

- Seventy-nine percent of people who attend church came because a friend or relative invited them.

- The top two "projection" factors are the church sign and the church website.

- We must strive for excellence in print.

CREATE POSITIVE FIRST IMPRESSIONS

"...for man looketh on the outward appearance, but the
LORD looketh on the heart."—1 SAMUEL 16:7

D uring the research phase of this book, we had the opportunity to visit many healthy churches. Our initial impression of the people and facilities was generally very good. It reinforced for us the importance of creating positive first impressions. Quite simply— growing and healthy churches are places where "all things are made ready" for guests when they arrive.

Scripture makes it clear that appearance matters to the Lord, because it is what men see! In Luke 14:16–17 we see this principle, "Then said he [Jesus] unto him, A certain man made a great supper, and bade many: And sent his servant at supper time to say to them that were bidden, Come; for all things are now ready." Think about that phrase "all things are now ready." In this parable, a great supper was prepared—and all the things pertaining to hosting that supper and receiving guests were made ready before the guests arrived. Think of the planning, the details, and the effort that would have gone into such a "great supper." Think of the Master who has commanded His servants to consider every detail in making a great feast and all things pertaining to that feast "ready" for His guests.

While we know the Lord is not impressed with outward appearance, we also know that Jesus was masterful at making "out of this world" first impressions. He began his earthly ministry by turning water into wine at a wedding feast! He fed thousands with a few loaves and fishes. He healed, amazed, and ministered to multitudes. He calmed seas, raised the dead, and cast out devils—all pretty positive and impressive deeds. He drew people to Himself like no other man could ever hope to do!

No, God isn't impressed with surface appearances, but the Scripture makes it clear that appearances can bring glory to Him. He reminds us that first impressions do matter to people. Matthew 12:23, "And all the people were amazed, and said, Is not this the son of David?" God instructs us with statements like these: "But ye are a chosen generation, a royal priesthood, an holy nation, a peculiar people; that ye should **shew forth** the praises of him who hath called you out of darkness into his marvellous light" (1 Peter 2:9). "Let your light so shine before men, that they may see your good works, and glorify your Father which is in heaven" (Matthew 5:16). What does it truly mean to "shew forth" His praises or His salvation? Clearly it is visible and has something to do with the impression we make upon others.

We will see later, this is not simply for the sake of impressing—but it is about a first impression with substance—an impression that flows forth from substantive reality for the glory of God. When people approach our property and enter our buildings, what they see and experience speaks volumes about how much we value our Lord and the privilege of worshipping in His house.

One of the most enlightening Bible illustrations with regard to positive first impressions is when the queen of Sheba came to "check out" Solomon and the God he served. First Kings 10:1 says, "And when the queen of Sheba heard of the fame of Solomon concerning the name of the LORD, she came to prove him with hard questions."

The queen of Sheba is a classic example of the power of "word of mouth" communication. She was so intrigued by what she heard about Solomon and his God that she had to see for herself. Many churches work hard to bring guests to church, only to see the guests never return. What turns them off? We would like to think it is the straight and strong preaching—and sometimes that is the case but not as often as we might think.

I (CR) remember a church I visited years ago. I was a teenager on my way to youth camp and had heard a really good report about the church's pastor and his burden for people. It was an especially hot day, and when I arrived at the church, I was overcome by the stench of manure. At first I thought the smell was a farm truck passing on the highway, but then I discovered a pig pen next to the church! As if the unbearable smell was not bad enough, there was the added sight of huge, sloppy hogs wallowing next to the Sunday school building! A church staff member later told me that it was the pastor who was raising the hogs. Even after all these years, I still vividly recall the pastor with the big heart and the stopped-up nose.

Can you imagine if you were to visit that church for the first time as a lost person or prospective member? You would wonder what in the world was going on! How could the pastor and members of that church not be embarrassed by the pig sty?

Over time, we can become desensitized to first impressions. The first day I (CR) worked as a package handler at a well-known shipping company, I was shocked at how people treated the boxes. Containers were thrown, dropped, kicked, and smashed. The "fragile" sticker on the side seemed to be an invitation for additional punishment! The first week I was so careful, but over time I grew less and less aware of how the people around me abused the packages and even began treating the boxes roughly myself.

That is how it is in real life, even in the church. Creating a positive first impression requires a constant, intentional "first look" refocusing— seeing our church all over again through the eyes of our guests. We must take nothing for granted. Things slip off the radar over time—even issues as major as the sight and smell of a pig sty on a hot day!

Have you ever asked someone who knows nothing about your church to visit and elaborate on their first impressions? Were the facilities well cared for? Were the people genuinely warm and welcoming? Was the service well prepared and thought through? Did the music and message speak to the heart? Many of us would be reluctant to ask questions like these because we would not want to hear the answers.

When the queen of Sheba visited Solomon, she came to "prove him." When people visit our churches for the first time, they often are "proving" us and our faith as well. What an opportunity! We must not underestimate how much is at stake in that first visit.

Notice what happened when the queen visited: "And when the queen of Sheba had seen all Solomon's wisdom, and the house that he had built, And the meat of his table, and the sitting of his servants, and the attendance of his ministers, and their apparel, and his cupbearers, and his ascent by which he went up unto the house of the LORD; there was no more spirit in her" (1 Kings 10:4–5).

The queen was speechless. She was wildly impressed. *Solomon's preparation of God's house was more than manipulation.* His efforts were so well done that the word of mouth actually understated its magnificence! Look at the queen's response in verse 7: "Howbeit I believed not the words, until I came, and mine eyes had seen it: and, behold, the half was not told me: thy wisdom and prosperity **exceedeth** the fame which I heard."

Solomon's "word of mouth" projection was honest and understated. The queen surely was excited about visiting, but she was blown away by the actual experience! Are discerning people ever "blown away" when they visit your church? Are they welcomed and loved beyond expectation? Are they surprised by the friendly spirit? Are they delighted by the reception they receive and the preparations that have been made for them?

Some churches have awesome advertising and slick websites or brochures, but when a person visits they are sincerely let down. This is the classic "style over substance" disappointment. While in the last chapter we talked about the church having a standard of excellence in outreach—how much more important is it that our guests' first experience delivers a higher standard of excellence? How valuable are *exceeded expectations* when it comes to preparing a heart to respond to the Gospel?

Solomon and his staff far exceeded the queen's expectations. We realize we are not in the entertainment business, and we're not called to merely "please men." Our calling and responsibilities, in fact, are much higher than entertainment or pleasure, yet often the world does a much better job of presenting or packaging itself (and for far lesser causes). Like an embassy on foreign soil, our churches represent Jesus and His presence on this earth. Wouldn't you be embarrassed if you went to a foreign country and realized the American embassy was the ugliest and worst-kept building on the street?

Notice the five areas in the text where a great first impression was made on the queen:

HE ANSWERED HER QUESTIONS

His speaking was "full of wisdom." "…and when she was come to Solomon, she communed with him of all that was in her heart. And Solomon told her all her questions: there was not any thing hid from the king, which he told her not" (1 Kings 10:2–3).

When people visit your church for the first time, are their questions fully and sincerely answered? These answers begin with simple things like where to park, how to find nurseries and classes, and whether someone feels welcomed and received. Directional signage, greeters, and well-trained ushers do much to help a first-time visitor become comfortable with new surroundings. Drive up to your church with the mindset of a first-time guest and start asking questions: Where do you go? What is the service schedule? Where is the service held? Are there opportunities for children and teens? These questions should be easily answered and clearly discerned.

Beyond this, what kind of reception do first-time guests receive? Are they welcomed with warmth and compassion? Consider James 3:17, "But the wisdom that is from above is first pure, then peaceable, gentle, and easy to be intreated, full of mercy and good fruits, without partiality, and without hypocrisy."

Pure. Peaceable. Gentle. Easy to be intreated. Full of mercy. Good fruit. No partiality. No hypocrisy. These are challenging words as we seek to contend with a culture that is less and less "Christian." Consider the Apostle Paul who said in 1 Thessalonians 2:7, "But we were gentle among you, even as a nurse cherisheth her children."

THE HOUSE OF GOD WAS IMPRESSIVE

"And when the queen of Sheba had seen all Solomon's wisdom, and the house that he had built…" (1 Kings 10:4).

Most of us do not have the vast resources of Solomon with which to build a home and house of worship as he did. All of us, however, can make the place God has given us respectable and clean.

Have you ever walked into an older hotel that was not well cared for? Did you notice the décor? The wear and tear? The smell? Then you enter a new hotel and notice a vastly higher standard of excellence. What a difference! Many Baptist churches desperately need to remove old paneling, repaint walls, repair carpet, and update furniture. In the eyes of a first-time guest, the condition of our place of worship reflects on our God and the reverence we have for Him.

The typical excuse for poorly prepared sanctuaries in struggling churches is finances. And yet, how could we ever expect the financial situation to improve if we aren't caring well for what God has provided? Why should we expect people to faithfully invest in that for which we show little value?

THE SERVANTS WERE LOVING AND HOSPITABLE

"And the meat of his table, and the sitting of his servants, and the attendance of his ministers…" (1 Kings 10:5).

In 1 Timothy 3:2, preachers are commanded, "A bishop then must be blameless, the husband of one wife, vigilant, sober, of good behaviour, **given to hospitality…."**

A church's hospitality begins with the example set by leadership. This is about the spirit of the pastor and staff. Are we allowing negative attitudes, lack of preparation, or other oversights to hinder the growth of our church? Is your spirit positive, warm, and genuinely loving and receptive?

Many pastors are given to a spirit of negativity or discouragement. Whether it's about someone leaving the church or some issue in culture, we tend to become critical or cynical. Our spirit ceases to be "contending for the faith" and it becomes "contentious in the faith." Rather than "striving together for the faith," we find ourselves striving against God's good work in the hearts of people.

Jesus loved people. We see His heart revealed in Matthew 9:36: "But when he saw the multitudes, he was moved with compassion on them, because they fainted, and were scattered abroad, as sheep having no shepherd."

There isn't a lot of love in today's secular culture, and when guests arrive on your campus and experience the genuine love of Christ flowing from the pastor, the staff, and the church family, it creates a powerful first impression. The love of Christ is compelling. It attracts and draws men toward the truth. John 13:35 reminds us, "By this shall all men know that ye are my disciples, if ye have love one to another." This sort of compassion is not only a powerful first impression; it is the most compelling reason that people return again and again to healthy churches!

Jesus instructed us to lead through a spirit of service. This is not about structuring your ministry around the "felt-needs" of people, but rather remembering that Jesus felt the needs of people and ministered to those needs. To serve people, you must be with them and expend yourself on their behalf. This is far more than a pulpit presence. It is the practice of giving yourself in sacrifice and sincerity.

Staying in the office until the last minute before service and leaving the sanctuary as the service is dismissed is not true hospitality. Darting out of church and heading home as quickly as possible and never opening up your home to guests and new Christians is not hospitality or a servant's spirit.

We need to relearn the importance of gracious hospitality. Welcoming guests—into our churches and into our lives—must be a key focus and a top priority. It must be a paradigm, not a surface experiment. We cannot be hermit ministers and expect that our church family will automatically respond to our leadership or visitors be blessed by our services.

For instance, I (PWC) and our staff make it a regular practice to invite church family members and new Christians to our homes for fellowship after Sunday evening services. Some time ago we moved our Sunday night service thirty minutes earlier, in part to allow for these important times of hospitality and life-building.

Moreover, hospitality must extend into our homes. Scripture demonstrates that Jesus spent much time mingling with people, even dining and celebrating in their homes. While He made sure He had time alone and while He was busy with ministry much of the time, He nevertheless made social interaction an important part of His ministry efforts.

THE DETAILS WERE WELL PREPARED

"And the meat of his table, and the sitting of his servants, and the attendance of his ministers, and their apparel, and his cupbearers..." (1 Kings 10:5).

Not everybody notices details. But everybody *feels* details! Everybody experiences them, whether they realize it consciously or not. The queen of Sheba both experienced and noticed the details:

How Solomon's servants were seated or arranged (etiquette)

The servants' attentiveness (attention to her needs and desires)

The clothing the servants wore

The people who provided security—the cupbearers

Given the big picture, some of these details seem minor. But the queen was impressed by the small things! Small thing speak loudly. Little things done well give your guests a greater confidence in the big things.

Jesus reminds us that He wants faithfulness in the little things: "He that is faithful in that which is least is faithful also in much…" (Luke 16:10).

Our family (CR) recently took an anniversary trip to the Four Seasons Aviara in northern San Diego, California. Now I have stayed in hotels all over the world, but a great hotel is about details. When my wife and I were checking in, the person at the counter asked for the name of our baby girl. I thought they were just listing her on the reservation for security purposes. Five minutes later, however, when we arrived at the room, we found a beautiful gold plate full of candy, artistically arranged around the letters "A-B-B-Y." In another five minutes, hotel staff carried in a crib, decked out in elaborate little girl décor and complete with toys for her to keep. The staff smiled broadly, anticipated our needs, and seemed to be obsessed with our comfort. I have been in nicer hotels, but never have I experienced a hotel where the staff cared so much about details.

Indeed, this is the goal. Positive first impressions are the first step to sharing Christ with a lost soul. Think of it this way—someone who doesn't like you isn't going to listen to you. If your first impression is negative, you've severely damaged your future efforts to share the Gospel.

THE WORSHIP WAS POWERFUL

"…and his ascent by which he went up unto the house of the LORD" (1 Kings 10:5).

The procession to the temple wowed the queen of Sheba. This procession was only one portion of the worship ceremony, but it was executed in such a way that a visitor said, "They were only walking from point A to point B, getting ready to worship, but it was such a sight to behold." If Solomon's procession was that enjoyable, can you imagine what the worship service was like?

Our worship services need to reflect the fact that we are entering the presence of Almighty God, Creator of the universe. Unfortunately, they many times come off flat and "hokey." Five minutes before the church service begins, someone is doing a microphone check, the special-music team is practicing their song for the first time, and the preacher is in his

EASTLAND BAPTIST CHURCH

TULSA, OKLAHOMA

Pastor Troy Dorrell states, "We must make the most of every guest who comes to Eastland." Rather than bemoan his challenges in having an older building in a rougher part of town, Pastor Dorrell decided to lead his church family to aggressively tackle the first impressions and early experiences of guests to their church services.

It began with regular coaching! Pastor Dorrell takes time during evening church services, in addition to his Bible message, to coach his church family—not merely in being friendly—but in actually *caring* for people. He says, "Being friendly is about a quick smile or a handshake—but *caring for people* is about helping them and nurturing them." In addition to "in-service" coaching, he has written articles on his pastoral blog to equip his church family in genuine care and compassion.

Pastor Dorrell also instituted a ministry called "The Guest Reception Ministry"—three separate teams of people who are responsible for helping guests have a wonderful and positive first experience at Eastland. When a guest arrives, the *parking lot team* meets them at the car. If it's raining, they have umbrellas. They welcome guests with warmth and then show them to the church lobby. (This team also rotates to provide campus security during the services.)

The Eastland lobby was deliberately designed for spacious areas of fellowship. Throughout, there are seating areas with floor rugs, sofas, and chairs. These areas provide a welcoming and comfortable atmosphere where people are encouraged to stay and fellowship. The lobby also features two welcome centers. As the parking team escorts guests to the welcome centers, they are met by *hosts*.

Hosts are more than greeters. While greeters at many churches are responsible for "greeting," hosts at Eastland are responsible to care for guests throughout their visit. The first thing a host does is present each guest with a welcome packet. This packet includes a booklet about the church and a visitor card, which the host asks the guest to fill out on the spot. Eastland is seeing 95% of their guests fill out information cards at the welcome center, as opposed to only 60% who filled them out when guests were welcomed in services.

A host will meet your entire family, walk you to nurseries, children's classes, adult classes, and even to the church service. After the service, the hosts are waiting in the lobby to answer questions or help in any way needed. This "hosting" is not overbearing, but sensitive. If a guest prefers not to be hosted, there's no pressure.

The third part of the guest reception ministry is the *ushers*. These men are responsible for helping people find seats and generally assisting with the flow of the service, etc.

When it comes to children's areas and youth classes, Pastor Dorrell stated that this was a "work in progress." They've tried to make each classroom bright and colorful. The children's classes have murals on the walls, and the workers are well-trained and friendly. The nurseries are clean, and the workers have been trained and taught how to welcome new mothers and alleviate their fears.

Regular training times are a significant part of each of these aspects of ministry. Pastor Dorrell and others are diligently equipping others in how to care for people of every age group as they arrive at Eastland Baptist Church.

This is one pastor and church family that has seriously evaluated the drawbacks of an older building design—and worked hard to compensate for those challenges. He states, "Our building is just not very user-friendly to a first-time guest. It's an old design that is difficult to navigate and find your way around. This gave us a compelling reason to develop our guest reception ministry."

First impressions make a difference, and Eastland Baptist Church is laboring to help new people successfully enjoy their first experiences with the church family!

office scrambling to finish his re-hashed outline. To a first-time guest, it comes off like "The Amateur Hour." Can you imagine that sort of last-minute scrambling for the opening ceremony of the Olympics? Yet our services are infinitely more important. Let us endeavor to make them the most creative, well thought out, and inspiring moments of the week.

Our experience in visiting the healthy churches in our research revealed well-prepared worship services. This isn't about being contemporary in music, carnal in presentation, or wordly in style. Quite the opposite—it is about truly and biblically reflecting the holiness and majesty of God and lifting hearts to focus upon Him. In growing churches, the music and preaching services are clearly pre-planned, rehearsed, and carefully thought through—from the testing of equipment, to the attire of singers, to the spoken words between songs and during prayers. The buildings are clean, bright, and inviting. The music is energetic, inspiring, and Christ-centered.

Our guests don't expect us to perform or to mimic popular late-night talk shows in our worship services; but they do deserve a genuine, well planned experience in God's presence with God's people. (1 Corinthians 14:40, "Let all things be done decently and in order.") Entertainment growth isn't healthy growth. But be sure—healthy churches have carefully planned services that honor the Lord and speak to the heart. These Christ-honoring first impressions go a long way toward encouraging a guest to return.

THE HOUSE OF GOD WAS A JOYFUL PLACE

"Happy are thy men, happy are these thy servants, which stand continually before thee, and that hear thy wisdom" (1 Kings 10:8).

God's people should be happy people—happy about their God, happy about serving in God's house, happy about hearing God speak. The happiness of people in our churches cannot be underestimated when it comes to first impressions. We're not talking about a kind of forced happiness or fakery. The queen of Sheba saw a genuine heart-happiness that manifested itself on the faces and in the lives of the people before the king.

How could people be so happy? In the same way that we are delighted after enjoying a good meal, we are happy when we have been served a heaping portion of wisdom! Proverbs 3:13 says, "Happy is the man that findeth wisdom, and the man that getteth understanding." The king's messages spoke to the people in such a way that their questions were answered and their hearts were filled with God's joy.

"Thou wilt shew me the path of life: in thy presence is fulness of joy; at thy right hand there are pleasures for evermore" (Psalm 16:11). There should be no happier place in your city than your local church! The joy of Christ is one of the most attractive qualities of a spirit-filled, thriving local church body. One hundred ninety-two times God chooses to use the word *rejoice* in Scripture! "Rejoice in the Lord alway: and again I say, Rejoice" (Philippians 4:4).

Let us pray that our local churches might exhibit the true joy of Jesus Christ! Let us preachers pray that God will give us such wisdom to impart to others, truths that will fill them up and encourage them to serve. May the result be a people who display a genuine, heartfelt happiness that guests cannot help but notice. This makes for an unforgettable first impression.

Let's evaluate the "first impression" of our services, church, sermons, and people by these criteria:

Is our speaking helpful and full of wisdom?

Is the house impressive?

Are we full of hospitality?

Do we pay attention to details?

Is our service excellent?

Is there joy among the servants?

The queen fell in love with what was going on in Solomon's ministry. Notice her response in verses 9–10:

"Blessed be the Lord thy God, which delighted in thee, to set thee on the throne of Israel: because the Lord loved Israel for ever, therefore made he thee king, to do judgment and justice. And she gave the king an hundred and twenty talents of gold, and of spices very great store, and precious stones: there came no more such abundance of spices as these which the queen of Sheba gave to king Solomon."

The queen gave praise to God and bestowed her treasures on Solomon. She was a changed woman! Oh, that our guests would be so deeply moved! What a shame for us to work so hard to get someone to the house of God, only to have him tune out before he ever even hears what we have to say. Bad first impressions undo all of God's good work before it ever happens. Most people decide to return or not to return to your church long before they ever hear the preacher.

Creating positive first impressions is about getting out of the way and letting God speak for Himself. It's about removing the distractions so that Christ, not our oversights, has the preeminence. We understand that, in spite of appearances, God knows the true condition of each heart, but people start on the outside and work their way in. Often, first impressions determine whether they will stay around long enough to hear the truth.

The principles of which we are speaking deal with the subject of *identification*. As a church, either your community will brand you, or you will brand yourself. There are always enemies of the church who will brand you in a way that is unbiblical and hurtful. We must be constantly counteracting and proactively projecting a biblical and accurate image of the Lord, our church, and our mission—to our community and to our guests.

As a local church, we must identify our own ministry—both in our projection and in our first impressions. Your church will either be the *friendly, fundamental, family-oriented* church in town, or you will be *the uncaring, isolated "cult"*—and it depends on who talks the most (and the most effectively) and how well you think through your first impressions. You must be the loudest voice in your community establishing in hearts and minds who you are and what you are about—and that impression should be positive and compassionate when guests arrive. If our message is offensive, we will stay true to the Cross. But if our spirit to care and nurture needs to improve, we must be willing to adjust.

CHAPTER SIX
TAKE–AWAYS

- Appearances can glorify God.

- First impressions often determine whether a guest will stay long enough to hear the truth.

- God commands us to "shew forth" His praises.

- Creating positive first impressions requires a constant intentional "first look."

- Healthy churches strive to exceed people's expectations.

- Healthy churches receive guests well and answer questions.

- Healthy churches are "given to hospitality."

- Positive first impressions come from excellence in the details.

- Healthy churches put much effort into well-planned worship services.

- Healthy churches are joyful places.

- Positive first impressions are about getting out of God's way and letting Him speak for Himself.

CONNECT GOD'S WORD WITH HEARTS

"But made himself of no reputation, and took upon him
the form of a servant, and was made in the likeness of
men: And being found in fashion as a man, he humbled
himself, and became obedient unto death, even the
death of the cross."—PHILIPPIANS 2:7–8

No one ever went to such great lengths as Jesus did to connect with lost people. He not only used the familiarities of everyday life to illustrate the Gospel's eternal truths, He even laid aside the glory of Heaven to become one of us!

We've seen that healthy churches reach out to their communities and compel guests to come to God's house. We've seen that they give great attention to the details of first impressions—that the hearts of guests might be softened and receptive to the message of the Gospel. Now, let's turn our hearts to the feast itself. Is there a difference between the feast prepared at healthy churches and the feast prepared at struggling churches?

The professional research team that studied the results of our survey identified *one characteristic* of preaching and teaching that had a high level of correlation in all growing churches. This characteristic plays out in two specific ways. To our research team, this finding was absolutely huge. Let's examine it in more detail.

PRACTICAL BIBLE PREACHING

Pastors who more frequently organize their sermons around a question, decision, or reality from today's context using one or more Scriptures to examine the theme *exhibit significantly more growth* than those who do this less often. This is very big.

In other words, pastors who connect the Bible with people's hearts in their preaching are much more likely to pastor growing churches. These pastors connect by using a touchstone in their listener's daily life and by showing how Scripture reveals God's wisdom for that area of life. They are practical about showing God's plan for saving us from the power and penalty of our sin.

President John Adams voiced this sentiment over two-hundred years ago when he said, "It is the duty of the clergy to accommodate their discourses to the times, to preach against such sins as are most prevalent, and recommend such virtues as are most wanted."

Interestingly, the style of preaching (expository, topical, etc.) did not affect the responses of those who heard the Gospel, as long as the pastor endeavored to frame biblical preaching in a way that connected with the lives and hearts of the hearers. This is solid biblical content well applied to practical everyday living. It is more than a delivery style, a personality attribute, or good communication skills. It is a burden and passion to connect life changing Bible truth to lives that need to be changed.

We see this example over and over in Scripture—in the ministry of Jesus, the apostles, and in the very nature of the Gospels. Consider the actual writing of the different Gospels:

The Writings of the Gospels

	Matthew	Mark	Luke	John
Primary Audience	Jews	Romans	Gentiles	Greeks
Portrait of Jesus	Jewish Messiah and King	Faithful servant	Perfect Man	God
Jesus' Genealogy	Traces genealogy to David. A king must have one.	None. A servant needs none.	Traces genealogy to Adam. A man needs one.	None. God has none.
Style of Writer	Teacher	Preacher	Historian	Theologian

While we understand that all the Gospels are given to *us*, we recognize they were written in such a way to connect with different groups at the time. The Gospels are four separate witnesses to the same events, much like the evening newscasts differ in emphasis because the news organizations report the same events with different audiences in mind.

We also see this in the preaching of Jesus. He took timeless, eternal truth and presented it in packages that common men could receive. He told stories to which average people could relate. In Mark 12:37 the Bible says, "…And the common people heard him gladly."

But Jesus did more than just connect well with the common people. He also discussed technical, theological matters with professional teachers in a way they could understand the truth He wanted to communicate. At twelve years old, Jesus was astounding doctors and lawyers with His teaching. In others words, whether the people were ordinary folks or highly educated sophisticates, Jesus connected with them where they were.

Paul operated in much the same manner. When he arrived in town, Paul always went straight to the Jewish synagogue to reason from the Scriptures with the people there. Acts 17:2 says, "And Paul, as his manner was, went in unto them, and three sabbath days reasoned with them out of the scriptures." Paul knew how to connect with Jewish people.

But Paul also knew how to connect with non-Jews. When he preached on Mars' Hill to the citizens of Greece, he quoted poets who were well known to his audience. He used illustrations that helped him establish common ground with those who heard him. Paul even knew how to connect with Roman rulers and political elite. He nearly persuaded King Agrippa to become a Christian.

Modern day "seeker-sensitive" philosophies tend to emphasize the importance of being *relevant* to the audiences' everyday life. This often equates to watering down or even omitting truth that might be difficult to receive. Many in the contemporary church movement refuse to use biblical words, advocate the breaking down of doctrinal walls, and present a much more non-confrontational social gospel. This is NOT what we would endorse (Reference: *The Saviour Sensitive Church* by Paul Chappell and John Goetsch from www.strivingtogether.com). Connecting God's Word with hearts is not about changing or softening His truth—it is about making it understandable and practical to the lives of the hearers.

Unfortunately, many in the contemporary church movement shy away from confronting people with biblical truth and with the need to make hard choices. The result is that many gain a temporary hearing for their message, but fall short of truly making disciples. The message is lacking the vital substance that "effectually worketh." First Thessalonians 2:13 says, "For this cause also thank we God without ceasing, because, when ye received the word of God which ye heard of us, ye received it not as the word of men, but as it is in truth, the word of God, which effectually worketh also in you that believe."

On the other hand, some pastors boldly confront people with biblical truth and hard choices, but do not attempt to first connect with people's hearts or to make the truth practical to their daily lives. Their substance is solid, but their approach is thoughtless, brash, or seemingly disconnected to reality.

Both approaches—whether compromise or careless—are unscriptural and ignore one biblical precedent or the other. Healthy

SPOTLIGHTING CHURCHES THAT WORK

HARVEST BAPTIST CHURCH

PITTSBURGH, PENNSYLVANIA

Pastor Kurt Skelly has seen his church family at Harvest Baptist Church surge forward both numerically and spiritually, and he credits the power of the Word of God. When you visit Harvest Baptist, it's clear that God is developing strong Christians in this church family. Pastor Skelly explains it this way, "My preaching is very predictable. I build every message upon the content of a text. I typically preach expository messages that navigate a text line upon line. Every point explains the text."

He further explains, "Sometimes preachers use the Word of God as a means to an end, but people need the Word of God—they don't need our manipulation of it. They don't need a sermon-esque 'term-paper' that uses the Word of God for source material to prove our point. They need the Word of God to be the very substance and structure of our message."

The sermon preparation process begins late in the year as Pastor Skelly chooses a theme for his New Year preaching and teaching series. These directions are determined through prayer and careful seeking of the Lord's guidance. From there he begins preparing biblical messages with three simple aspects in mind—*Explain, Illustrate, and Apply* (EIA.) In each message he teaches, preaches, and pastors.

Explaining the text is where his role as a teacher comes through. He defines Bible words, explains the meanings of the passages, and expounds the historical and biblical context. He often uses the Bible to explain the Bible. His goal—to bring Bible passages into clarity for his church family and to help them think biblically, textually, and contextually.

In *illustrating* the text he generally finds himself preaching and asking God to "open a window and shine the light on the truth." He looks for and prayerfully asks God to provide creative illustrations or other Bible passages that can illuminate the hearts of the hearers. He also uses personal illustrations as the Lord leads.

In *applying* the truth, he is pastoring his church family. This is where the pastor's heart comes in—he knows and prays for the flock. He knows the audience, and he's thinking his way into their lives—the kids, the teens, the couples, the seniors, the people groups, the families. The application should never focus upon one individual but always consider the needs of every group. He works to take the truth of a passage and thematically and creatively address the needs of the people in every lifestage.

He says, "Biblical preaching must be a non-negotiable. Refuse to allow your preaching to become reactionary, and let it flow from a pre-planned direction. The pastor is preparing spiritual meals—and is responsible to prepare a healthy, well-balanced diet. We're not there to be spectacular or to 'wow' people with our favorite meal. We're there to provide a balanced diet, and the best way to do that is to systematically preach through the Bible with a steady menu of expository preaching."

The advantages of this approach? It forces the pastor to stay on Bible themes. It forces the pastor to stay in context as he preaches. And it literally teaches the church family to think biblically. This method of preaching indirectly teaches people how to study the Bible for themselves.

Pastor Skelly's admonition to preachers: "Derive your points from the text in context. There is a place for topical preaching when there is a special need, but as a diet, your church family needs the whole counsel of God."

Finally, Pastor Skelly pointed out that the pastor is responsible not only for his own preaching, but also the teaching of others. We must populate our lecterns with people who follow this same biblical method of textual preaching and teaching. The pastor must think of all of the teaching and preaching that happens throughout the church and insure that the people are getting a healthy and balanced diet at every age and in every class.

churches do not err to either of these extremes. They take the undiluted message of Scripture and make it intensely practical and personal for daily living.

In high school, I (CR) was a member of the marching band. Because we were performing on the field, we were unable to see or appreciate the formations we executed. We were always busy marching! Occasionally, however, we were able to watch a video tape of the performance. I was always amazed at what the formations looked like from the grandstand.

But even then, we were just seeing the dispassionate view of a camera stationed at one specific location in the stands. Different viewers in the grandstand saw the performance in different ways. Some of the audience were so intoxicated they could not care less about what the band was doing. Some in the crowd were tone deaf and could not appreciate the music. Some parents thought everything their child did was great —even if that child was out of step and off key. But then there were *the judges.* Using their technical expertise, their job was to critically evaluate every move that was made and every song that was played.

The band director had to deal with the uneasy tension of satisfying both the judges and the crowd. Some marching bands were all about pleasing the crowd. They only played popular songs, and every song was performed loudly. The crowds loved them! The judges, on the other hand, were not impressed.

Some bands were all about the judges. They played an odd assortment of unfamiliar songs and choreographed the band in a strange mix of shapes and colors. The judges loved them—but no one in the stands wanted to hear these bands. People would literally leave their seats at halftime looking for anything else to do just to avoid hearing these bands.

Our challenge as Bible preachers is to both please the Judge and connect with the audience. In every respect, the Judge must be pleased. Our preaching of the Gospel must please the Judge. Paul said it like this: "But as we were allowed of God to be put in trust with the gospel, even so we speak; not as pleasing men, but God, which trieth our hearts"

(1 Thessalonians 2:4). There can be no compromise on the absolute, eternal truth of the Gospel message.

But our Judge understands that the Gospel is also to a crowd. The marching band's judges did not care one whit whether the delivery engaged the crowd. Our Judge, however, is not pleased with an empty house. He loves "the crowd"—He is passionate about lost humanity. He is grieved when people wander off without understanding the depth of His love for them and the awful price He paid for their salvation. What does it profit if we have the right message and empty seats?

When it comes to preaching, the man of God must not shy away from the truth or limit the scope of the Gospel. But neither should he allow the Gospel to be hidden under a bushel. For the Gospel is effectively obscured when the hearers do not understand or connect the message with their everyday lives.

Healthy churches have pastors who diligently labor in the Word of God to connect it to the hearts and lives of the hearers. But there is a second aspect of this finding that is also consistently found in strong churches.

AGE-SPECIFIC, LIFE-SPECIFIC MINISTRY

The pastors of healthy and growing churches agreed that their churches were:

1. *Effective at reaching young adults*
2. *Effective at reaching families with children*
3. *Effective at reaching senior adults*

In every case, these churches exhibit significantly higher levels of worship attendance growth. What does this tell us?

Healthy churches make a concerted effort to connect God's Word with *all* age groups or community subgroups. Pastors and teachers in these churches make intentional efforts to present the Gospel in terms that each age group in the church and each segment of their community can understand. Subgroups in the neighborhood are not ignored or shunned.

For instance—healthy churches are sensitive to ethnic populations in their communities, and they are starting ministries to those groups in their own languages. They would be more likely to establish a class for single mothers or one for ladies whose husbands do not attend church. They would be more likely to consider having ministries to those with specific challenges such as sinful addictions. They might adjust the weekly service schedule in light of the needs of their region.

Beyond the consideration of subgroups, these churches are also age specific in ministry. Regardless of their size, they have focused ministry to children, teens, singles, couples, and seniors. The planning and preparation of these ministries is not about entertainment or pleasing an age-group—but rather about specifically connecting God's truth to the hearts and practical needs of every age.

Unfortunately, there seems to be a growing trend in our independent Baptist ranks to adopt a "refuge" mentality. Rather than identifying segments of our community that are not being reached with the Gospel and figuring out how to communicate the Gospel in ways they can understand, some are retreating behind the church walls and simply continuing to "preach to the choir." Souls are lost because we refuse to move beyond our comfort zone and take the Gospel into the cultures of outsiders.

Consider the Apostle Paul's approach to reaching people:

"For though I be free from all men, yet have I made myself servant unto all, that I might gain the more. And unto the Jews I became as a Jew, that I might gain the Jews; to them that are under the law, as under the law, that I might gain them that are under the law; To them that are without law, as without law, (being not without law to God, but under the law to Christ,) that I might gain them that are without law. To the weak became I as weak, that I might gain the weak: I am made all things to all men, that I might by all means save some. And this I do for the gospel's sake, that I might be partaker thereof with you" (1 Corinthians 9:19–23).

Paul declared:

I will become like a Jew to reach a Jew.
I will become like a Gentile to reach a Gentile.
I will become like the weak to reach the weak.

Isn't this precisely what a missionary does when he goes to a foreign culture? Don't we expect the missionary to learn the language of the people he is trying to reach? Don't we ask him to make every reasonable accommodation with regard to the other cultures in ways that do not dishonor God? Do we expect the people there to learn English and wear ties in order to hear the Gospel? Of course not. Our missionaries learn the language or use an interpreter to proclaim the truth of the Gospel in a way the hearers can understand. Culturally, missionaries eat the food and accommodate to the culture in every way that does not violate Scripture. That is how the Gospel makes its way into a new culture and begins to multiply in an indigenous way throughout the population.

As America becomes more and more post-Christian, we are going to have to begin thinking of America as a mission field. Healthy churches are seeing this and responding accordingly. We are certainly not saying we must grow out our hair, pierce our tongues, and abandon our standards of biblical separation, but cultural isolationism is just as dangerous as over-contextualization. The fruit of one is compromise; the consequence of the other is the inability to reach people.

Consider what Jesus did to connect with people where they were:

"But made himself of no reputation, and took upon him the form of a servant, and was made in the likeness of men: And being found in fashion as a man, he humbled himself, and became obedient unto death, even the death of the cross" (Philippians 2:7–8).

Jesus allowed Himself to be made in the "likeness" of men. Can you imagine how radical a sacrifice that was for Him? He grew weary; He experienced hunger; He felt pain; He suffered death. He journeyed from the perfect glory of Heaven to the womb of a sinner named Mary. And while He was here, Jesus even aggravated the isolationists by eating with "sinners."

We must consider the implications of the incarnation as we think about connecting with the hearts of people who are not being reached in our communities with the Gospel. We must remember the extremes to which Jesus was willing to go that He might connect with us and redeem us from our sin.

THE PRIORITY OF BIBLE PREACHING AND TEACHING

The preaching or teaching platforms of your local church represent God's chosen method of touching humanity with His eternal truth. The pastor and the teachers in those environments have a great gift—the responsibility of communicating God's truth. In some cases the listeners are English speaking or perhaps Spanish speaking. In some cases they are very young and in others, very old. Some of our listeners are starting families, others are building businesses. Some are struggling with addiction, others are recovering from divorce. Many are searching for answers to everyday life. It is the unbearable emptiness and the daily discomfort of those nagging needs that often compel them to come to us in search of answers.

Do we connect God's answers with those hearts? Do we make God's truth applicable and practical? Do we answer their questions, fill their hearts, and feed their souls with God's powerful Word?

The privilege of teaching and preaching God's Word is a great gift—we must use it well. Our preaching is the great and high calling of God upon our lives. It is not our primary responsibility to fill the pews of the church, but rather to fill the pulpit of the church—to make sure that we are preaching the whole counsel of God.

It is a great privilege and responsibility to stand in the pulpit of a New Testament Baptist church and deliver the Word to open hearts.

In closing this chapter, I (PWC) would like to share a few practical applications on connecting God's Word with the hearts of people:

First, preach and teach contextually. This is a pastor or teacher who preaches the text and develops it historically and accurately. We must do everything we can to help people understand the text of the Bible and how it affects their lives today.

Second, immerse yourself in the Scriptures. Create time to deliberately contemplate and meditate on your text. Rightly divide God's truth, and make it real to the people who hear you.

Third, carefully apply your preaching or teaching to your listeners. With children that might mean we use puppets and visuals. With adults it might mean using PowerPoint to show a Bible map or using illustrations as Jesus did with the parables. We must do everything we can to make the Bible come alive and to communicate God's truth in ways that make it memorable and helpful.

Fourth, develop scriptural sermon series. Either present the truth verse by verse, or support your topical message with many Scriptures, and explain them in a way that people can use throughout the week.

Fifth, preach consistent and clear Gospel presentations. When you do, avoid clichés like "turn your life over to Jesus." Don't be afraid to compel people to Christ, and don't merely present a social gospel.

Sixth, use Bible words and define them. Don't avoid the Bible—teach it. And yet, don't expect unsaved hearts to understand Bible words. We ostracize our guests by presuming that they understand culturally unfamiliar words.

Seventh, be sure to give a clear and compassionate invitation. Preaching should always compel men to make a decision. As we will see in chapter 10, healthy churches are not afraid to lovingly compel people to spiritual commitment.

People come back to a church where they received something that was useful in their lives—and nothing is more powerful, practical, and useful than the Word of God. It speaks to every need of the human heart, and it is always relevant throughout every age and cultural shift. This is not about compromising the truth and simply presenting pop-psychology, but rather about prayerful and biblical application that connects truth to the reality of our daily lives.

Take a moment and carefully consider your message. Is it biblical? Is it practical? It should be both. The Bible commands this; the needs of humanity compel this; and the research of healthy churches validates this. Strong churches have strong messages with practical and helpful application.

What next? What happens after a guest has been fed a practical and helpful meal from God's Word? What happens after our visitors leave our front doors?

In healthy churches, the work has just begun!

CHAPTER SEVEN
TAKE–AWAYS

- All healthy churches are focused on connecting God's truth to the hearts and lives of people.

- Undiluted scriptural content combined with intensely practical applications changes lives.

- Healthy churches are sensitive to different people groups.

- Healthy churches are sensitive to different age groups.

- Nothing can replace the power of God's Word flowing from an anointed pastor.

- Our church families are helped by solid biblical preaching that practically applies God's truth to everyday life.

- People return to a church where they received something useful.

FOLLOW UP BIBLICALLY AND STRATEGICALLY

"For ye remember, brethren, our labour and travail: for labouring night and day, because we would not be chargeable unto any of you, we preached unto you the gospel of God."—1 THESSALONIANS 2:9

What do farmers do after they prepare the soil and plant the seed? There is much work between sowing and reaping. They water the seed. They protect the crop from insects and infestations. They pull weeds that would overtake the seed. They repel animals and rodents that would damage the crop. They tend the fields and nurture growth.

And so it is in local church ministry. There is much labor that must take place to see "fruit that remains." For Jesus said in John 15:16, "Ye have not chosen me, but I have chosen you, and ordained you, that ye should go and bring forth fruit, and that your fruit should remain...." Our Master never intended for our work to be completed after a soul is saved or after a guest visits our church one time.

What happens to visitors after they leave your church? Do they hear from you? Do they feel welcome to visit again? Do they consistently return? Why or why not?

As the agricultural revolution changed farming forever, even so the technological and information age has provided tools and resources that greatly increase our potential to reach and disciple more people than ever before. Our follow-up can be more planned, more focused, and more strategic than ever before.

In our survey, several interesting facts rose to the surface when contrasting healthy churches with struggling churches. Struggling churches tended to agree with this statement: "It is a constant struggle to integrate new converts into our church." Healthy churches showed a strong trend the other direction.

The most significant observation pertaining to this chapter is this: *100% of the healthy churches we surveyed have a defined process for following up with visitors through mail, phone, email, or personal visits.*

Did you catch that statistic? 100%! This means that healthy and growing churches always—*ALWAYS*—have a biblical strategy for following up and building relationships with first-time guests. From church to church and region to region this strategy may vary slightly, but in healthy churches, it is *always* there.

If you were asked to produce a list of the last six months visitors to your church services—could you easily retrieve that list? Could you identify and quantify what efforts your church family has made to contact each guest and what the response was? Could you easily find out how many times they have been visited or called, what questions they had, whether they are saved and baptized, and how often they have returned (if at all)? Have you tracked their spiritual progress in any way?

It is surprising how many churches have no system or strategy in place for touching the lives of guests after the first visit. On a practical level, this is just bad management—ineffective stewardship. On a spiritual level, it could be considered outright disobedience.

Consider everything we have studied to this point in comparison with this one key factor. Many growing churches have good locations, nice facilities, colorful brochures, and positive first impressions—but not all churches. However, *all* growing churches follow-up on visitors. This is essential. And the more challenges you face in other areas, the more effective your follow-up must be. This factor can compensate for a host of other challenges such as limited advertising budgets or out of the way locations. A well-executed and biblical follow-up program is indispensable to bearing "fruit that remains."

What does this follow-up look like, and how does God bless it? Let's examine two aspects of follow-up—first the biblical pattern and then a practical strategy.

FOLLOW UP BIBLICALLY

No matter where you look in God's Word for patterns of follow-up, it boils down to hard work and personal sacrifice. This is where real ministry happens—one life touching one life at a time.

First Thessalonians 2:7–10 gives one of many biblical illustrations and instructions regarding the labor of the Apostle Paul in the lives of people. Read and consider his labor and investment:

"But we were gentle among you, even as a nurse cherisheth her children: So being affectionately desirous of you, we were willing to have imparted unto you, not the gospel of God only, but also our own souls, because ye were dear unto us. For ye remember, brethren, our labour and travail: for labouring night and day, because we would not be chargeable unto any of you, we preached unto you the gospel of God. Ye are witnesses, and God also, how holily and justly and unblameably we behaved ourselves among you that believe."

Paul's first priority was to share the Gospel, and he did so gently—cherishing the souls of the people he was reaching. Even so, the first priority of a follow-up program must be the sharing of the Gospel of Jesus Christ. Local church ministry can see a soul saved in a variety of contexts. Many are saved out in the community through door-to-door soulwinning before they ever visit the church. Others respond at church to an invitation or the leading of a friend to share the Gospel. Many others are saved after their first visit to church—through the follow-up of the church family. And some are saved weeks or months into their faithful attendance of a local church.

There is no biblical precedent that one or the other of these is in any way more significant. It truly depends on the work of the Holy Spirit within the heart of a lost man—and a good follow-up program will make room for all of these possibilities in order that the Holy Spirit, rather than a "strategy," may remain the prime mover.

Suffice it to say, at Lancaster Baptist, we see God work in different ways to bring many different lives to Christ. People are often led to Christ through our ministry, but God uses all of the processes above to bring them to salvation. Until someone has trusted Christ, however, we continue to follow-up with a salvation focus.

After salvation, we follow-up for baptism. This happens through personal visits and sharing biblical principles. We make every effort to compel a new Christian to follow in obedience to the Lord by being baptized into the church family and publicly identifying with Christ.

The Apostle Paul didn't stop at sharing the Gospel—he imparted his own soul. He gave himself. He labored and travailed night and day. He showed himself a pattern of biblical living. He obviously built sincere, loving relationships with those he led to Christ.

A good follow-up program doesn't stop at sharing Christ or compelling baptism. A good follow-up program builds relationships and connects the soul of a new convert to the souls of God's people in a local church. It establishes a new Christian in a new pattern of Christ-like living and provides a sense of belonging as a part of a local body.

In healthy churches, follow-up is more than a "thank you for visiting" letter. It is the beginning of a relationship, birthed out of love, developed through travail and personal labor, and fruitful over months and years. Do you have a strategy for such follow-up?

FOLLOW UP STRATEGICALLY

A dream without a plan is a wish. Without the right strategy, you will never fulfill the ministry to which God has called you. Most pastors and mature Christians dream of producing mature disciples of Christ. We long to be fruitful in the work of God, and yet we're often at a loss for exactly what steps to take. We fail to define the process, so our follow-up tends to be directionless and blurry at best.

A good follow-up strategy understands four principles:

The principle of orientation—how we orient new people to the ministry of our church, the principles of biblical living, and the process of growing in the local church. Could you or a faithful church member take out a blank piece of paper and quickly write out the process your church uses to build spiritually mature Christians? Is your church crystal clear about how you do the work of ministry? If not, your follow-up process is most likely struggling and vague. (We will study more in chapter 11 how a clearly stated purpose defines orientation.) For instance, if a mature Christian is making a follow-up visit to a saved visitor—what next? What is the next step forward spiritually? Are they invited to a special class? A fellowship? An orientation? Are they compelled to join a Sunday school class? Exactly what should be shared in the follow-up visit? Where is the guest directed?

There are many ways to orientate new Christians and prospective church members—but all healthy churches know "what is next." They've answered this question, put the answer into place, and educated the whole church family in sharing that step. Good follow-up programs know "what to share and how to share it."

The principle of segmentation—a strategy that allows your first-time guests to quickly and genuinely connect with people who are most like them. This ties in a bit to the "age-specific, life-specific" ministry mentioned in the last chapter but pertains primarily to follow up.

Think of it this way—the best prospects for faithful church membership are those people whom the Lord has led to visit your church. Once the question of salvation is settled, the glue that will connect a person to your church family for the long term is *relationships*. We realize that with mature Christians, the primary connection point should be doctrine, but healthy churches are reaching new souls and developing young Christians. And in the lives of new Christians, friendships and relationships—*love*—are the initial glue holding new converts to the

COASTLINE BAPTIST CHURCH

OCEANSIDE, CALIFORNIA

Pastor Stephen Chappell planted the Coastline Baptist Church in Oceanside, California, in 1998. The church recently celebrated its tenth anniversary in a newly remodeled building and consistently averages over 700 in weekly attendance. The Chappells moved to Oceanside completely by faith, and with the help of supporting churches they invested their hearts and lives into establishing a new church by faith.

Over the years, Pastor Chappell has been biblical and strategic in his follow-up of first-time guests, and he has led his church family in the same spirit. Their process of follow-up is creative, unique, and very effective. Nationally, about 14–16% of church visitors are likely to become church members. But Coastline is presently on track to see 25% of their first-time guests become faithful members this year. God is doing something special through the follow-up of this local body.

"This might surprise you," Pastor Chappell shares, "but we don't drop by unannounced, and we don't really try to get into the home after the first visit. We are passionate about seeing people saved, but we see many more saved by nurturing the process a little differently than most churches might think of at first."

The process is simple. After a first visit, the immediate goal is to express a gentle touch that invites the guest back for a second visit to church. "Our guests just aren't ready for a home visit right after their first time to our church. Many of them find that overwhelming." The church sends out a "thank you for visiting" email, followed by a Monday phone call from a secretary. The secretary usually leaves a voice mail courteously stating that someone will be dropping off a gift at their door on Tuesday night just to say, "Thanks for visiting."

At Tuesday night soulwinning, teams of people are each given a visitation card, a map, a fresh Marie Callenders' pie, and a personal

COASTLINE BAPTIST CONTINUED...

thank-you note from the pastor. The teams then leave the pies at the front door of every guest. Usually, little or no personal contact is made at this point. Obviously if the Lord opens the door, the teams are prepared to visit and share Christ. Pastor Chappell stated, "Delivering a pie actually makes follow-up a lot more enjoyable for our church family. They *love* taking pies to the homes of our guests!"

"Our guests are much more open to an in-home visit after their second time to our church. Many of them are asking questions and are eager to find out more about Christ and the church at that point," Pastor Chappell shared. Every Sunday, he makes a big deal out of first *and* second-time guests, and it's the *second-time* guests that are asked for a personal appointment.

The vast majority of people led to Christ at Coastline are won after the second visit to church during an in-home visit. Many of these are the same people who raised their hands during an invitation but were nervous about coming forward.

From an organizational standpoint, the church office maintains all of the guests in a tracking database. Families stay on this prospect list until they become members, until they ask to be taken off the list, or when they join another church. The goal is to get the family off of the prospect list and onto a Sunday school class roster—being followed up by a class teacher.

One pastoral staff member oversees this list and generally "pastors" it as though it were his own class. Each week, the results from follow-up visits are entered into this database, and Pastor Chappell reviews the reports of the visits.

"We're trying something new, but we're not sure how it's going to work out," Pastor Chappell shared. "Soon we're going to invite our guests to come to church fifteen minutes early for coffee in our café. We will invite them to come to this 'getting to know you' time for four weeks in a row—hoping to provide a more comfortable setting for fellowship. We believe this will be a 'next step' between visiting the church and becoming a part of an adult class."

church body. "By this shall all men know that ye are my disciples, if ye have love one to another" (John 13:35).

It stands to reason that retired couples connect better with other retired couples. Korean Christians enjoy fellowship with other Korean Christians. Teenagers look for other teenagers. And young families are seeking other young families for friendship and encouragement. We identify with those most like ourselves.

With this in mind—does your follow-up program quickly and genuinely connect new people with those in a similar lifestage? Do teens and teen workers follow-up on young people, young couples with young couples, singles with singles, and seniors with seniors? Obviously, this should all be at the pastor's discretion in assigning follow-up visits, and it's always a good idea for guests to connect with the heart of the pastor.

Simply put, good follow-up programs put careful thought into "who is following up on whom."

The principle of bonding—the understanding that follow-up helps people develop a bond with this new church family and new spiritual direction. I (PWC) often teach pastors that there are three dynamics happening in a person's journey from "visitor" to "faithful member" or "mature Christian."

Dynamic #1: Interfacing—all of the activity we covered in chapters 5 and 6. It is the outreach and first impressions of our church with potential visitors. Many times people don't attend church until after a fifth or sixth touch in this *interfacing* stage.

Dynamic #2: Bonding—the process of building a relationship with the church and church family. This is when our guests hear and enjoy the music and preaching. They are invited to your home for fellowship. They meet new people. They begin to experience authentic local church ministry on a personal level, and their hearts bond with the local body.

Dynamic #3: Ownership—when a person enrolls in a class, participates in discipleship, and grows in a feeling of ownership toward the church family and ministry. Ultimately this leads to a membership decision, and we pray, long-term spiritual growth.

Again, salvation could occur at any point in this process (though we believe that church membership should be reserved for saved, baptized Christians).

The principle of organization—actually creating and organizing a formal tracking and reporting system for all guest follow-up. It should be our passion that no soul would "fall through the cracks" and fail to be presented the opportunity to be saved and to grow in God's grace. Yet, in many churches, this is exactly what happens. The effort expended to reach the community and sow the seed ultimately breaks down as guests and prospects fall through the organizational cracks in the follow-up process.

Healthy churches seal up the cracks and make follow-up a neatly organized and systematic process. That is not to say it loses a personal touch or genuineness or the Holy Spirit's leading or guidance—simply that there is a structure to make sure that no one is overlooked.

Perhaps this will involve the pastor personally, a secretary, or an outreach director. Perhaps it will involve spreadsheets, databases, charts, or reporting forms. The systems will vary from church to church, but the commitment is constant in healthy churches.

On the following page I (pwc) am placing a chart that we have used at Lancaster Baptist Church for many years. This chart defines our strategy—the process by which we help our visitors become long-term church members.

You will see from this chart that we follow the initial contact or visitor's card through a series of checkpoints until the prospect has had the opportunity to hear the Gospel, be baptized, and ultimately become a member. This level of tracking is a corporate responsibility that the local body must take very seriously.

One of the key aspects of our follow-up program is the personal use of a prospect list. We encourage not only the church staff but the deacons and entire church family to keep such a list. This list is simply a way to keep track of individuals to whom you are witnessing and nurturing to the next level of their faith.

LifeStages Soulwinning Follow-Up Procedure

Visitor turns in visitor card at
Worship Service.

Visitor's information is
recorded on stat sheet.

Visitor information is entered
in database for tracking.

Visitor is assigned to staff or
class leader for follow-up.

*This assignment is based
on LifeStages (age-
divisions on visitor card
match class age-divisions).*

Follow-up visit is given to
leader with map attached.

Visit is made, and results are
reported to soulwinning secretary.

Visit information is entered
in database.

Status reports are given to
pastor, showing results of visits.

*These reports are
updated and given to
pastor twice a week.*

Visitor remains on leader's
prospect list until he becomes
a member.

For example, if I (pwc) receive a visitation card from the soulwinning director, make the visit on a Tuesday night and do not find the visitor at home, I will place him on my prospect list and continue following up on that individual until there has been a decision made for the Lord or the prospect becomes a "dead end."

As a pastor, along with our staff and key lay leaders, I have endeavored to build and maintain prospect lists for many years. The goal of a prospect list is to develop relationships with those we come in contact with or meet throughout the week. Yes, we will often attempt to lead them to Christ at a first meeting. But there are cases where we are briefly introduced to someone or present the Gospel without a person trusting Christ. In these cases, we will either write, visit, or give them a phone call each week. The goal is to consistently share the Gospel and follow-up with this person until he is saved and added to the church.

This process is a blend of *individual responsibility*—one Christian following up on one life at a time, and *corporate responsibility*—the entire church family loving, ministering to, and welcoming new Christians. We often send letters, emails, and follow-up information to recent guests, just as a loving nudge or ministry touch.

The point of this chapter is not to define your process of follow-up as much as it is to compel you to define it for your own local church. If you desire for your church to bear fruit, you must determine to follow up biblically and strategically.

A few years ago, I (pwc) was standing in the lobby after our morning service (my practice after every service). I was greeting our church family, praying with people, meeting guests, and trying to minister to needs. At one point a well-dressed couple from Africa stopped and shook my hand, introducing themselves as having recently relocated to America to study medicine. Having just preached the Gospel, I asked this man, Joseph, if he was sure that he was on his way to Heaven. With accented syllables he asked, "Can you know that?" He smiled when I said, "Yes you can." I then asked a faithful man in our church to sit down with Joseph and share Christ with him. Several moments later, Joseph met me in the lobby with a broad smile. His wife, who was already saved, was also smiling. He had just trusted Christ as his Saviour.

In that moment I invited Joseph and his wife to my home that evening for fellowship. We already had several church families and new Christians coming to our home that evening, and I knew that this would be a wonderful experience for this man and his wife. They graciously accepted, and later that evening, in the family room of my home, I introduced Joseph to others in our church family and asked him to share what had happened that morning.

With his beautiful accent, he shared the story of trusting Christ and having the assurance of eternal life. Across the room, the eyes of faithful longtime members and new members alike filled with tears and rejoiced in the grace of God upon this new believer. Joseph and his wife were welcomed into a family, and longtime members were strengthened and revived by the testimony of new life in Christ. As I stood there, I couldn't help but be overwhelmed by the presence of God and the greatness of His plan in authentic local church ministry.

Joseph and his wife are dear friends and members of our church to this day. They love the Lord and are grateful for the salvation in Christ and the acceptance in a church family that they found that day.

Healthy churches follow up—not merely with systems and strategies, but with biblical, Christ-like love and nurture. Charts and spreadsheets might help us organize the process, but the work is truly one of grace and Holy Spirit filling.

Well, our work still is not done. We may have reached out to the community, compelled guests to come to the banquet, provided good first impressions, and we may have even led a soul to Christ and helped him bond to our local body. There are still three more practices that healthy churches consistently implement from God's Word. Growing churches do more than attract people and reach them. They build them and keep them. While these past few chapters have been about "opening the front door" of the church, the next few chapters focus more on "closing the back door."

Let's examine the ongoing work of God in lives through local church ministry.

CHAPTER EIGHT
TAKE–AWAYS

- Healthy churches define a process for following up and tracking guests after their first visit.

- The biblical pattern of follow-up is personal, gentle, patient, and laborious.

- A good follow-up program builds relationships that grow over weeks, months, and years.

- A good follow-up program involves a predetermined strategy.

- Follow-up should orient people to the church, the Gospel, and the Christian life.

- Follow-up should allow people to meet the people in the church whom they are most like.

- A guest goes through three phases of relationship with a church—interfacing, bonding, and ownership.

- A good follow-up program develops individual responsibility that is accountable to a tracking system.

- Good follow-up is not just about systems, but rather about Christ-like love and nurture.

USE EFFECTIVE TOOLS AND TECHNOLOGIES

*"Where no oxen are, the crib is clean: but much increase
is by the strength of the ox."*—PROVERBS 14:4

The rapid advance of technology has swept our culture off its feet. The dizzying pace of change leaves little time for reflection on the moral impact of a new gadget or technical development. Those of us who care deeply about preserving and advancing godly values often find that a fad has penetrated society before we were even aware enough to raise a voice of protest.

There is, of course, nothing inherently evil about technology. Amazing advances in our tools create opportunities for tremendous good, even for God's Kingdom, as well as for great evil. What we need is some way to understand the impact of technology and discern its positive effects from the negative.

In *The Third Wave*, futurist Alvin Toffler identified three waves of change that dramatically changed the Western world over the past century and a half. Wave One was the *agricultural age,* in which people primarily worked the land, and life revolved around the farm. Today, fewer than 3% of Americans work on farms.

Wave Two was an *industrial age,* in which people used machines to increase productivity. Mechanical innovations transformed life in almost every respect. Printing, agriculture, manufacturing, and transportation were revolutionized. Jobs that once required hundreds of men now could be handled by one man and his machine. Trips that took months were reduced to hours. As a result, many Americans moved from farms to the cities to work in factories. Life in that age revolved around the factory, but today manufacturing jobs employ only 17% of the U.S. population.

Wave Three is our current *information or technological age,* in which people are primarily focused on accessing or exchanging information and experiences. The technological age began with the invention of the telephone and has surged stronger with the creation of the personal computer and the internet. The telephone penetrated the homes of 75% of the American population in seventy years; it took only seven years for the internet to achieve the same feat. Today a large percentage of American work revolves around a computer.

Look at how these waves have changed the farming industry throughout the past 150 years:

In **1850,** it took about *75 to 90* labor-hours to produce *100* bushels of corn on 2.5 acres by walking and using a plow, harrow, and hand planting.

In **1890,** it took about *35 to 40* labor-hours to produce *100* bushels of corn on 2.5 acres by walking and using a 2-bottom gang plow, disk and peg-tooth harrow, and a 2-row planter.

In **1945,** it took about *10 to 14* labor-hours to produce *100* bushels of corn on 2 acres using a tractor, 3-bottom plow, 10-foot tandem disk, 4-section harrow, 4-row planters and cultivators, and 2-row picker.

In **1987,** it took about *2.75* labor-hours to produce *100* bushels of corn on 1 1/8 acres using a tractor, 5-bottom plow, 25-foot tandem disk, planter, 25-foot herbicide applicator, 15-foot self-propelled combine, and trucks.[1]

More recently, information technologies have multiplied the efficiency of farm machines. A farmer can climb into his tractor, turn on the auto-pilot, and work his land with the assistance of GPS satellite technology and computer software. Perry Rust of Rust Sales, an agricultural company just outside Fargo, North Dakota, says a farmer in his tractor only needs to turn around at the end of the field. "The rest of the time, you're monitoring the air seeder or checking the yield monitor, answering the cell phone, or eating lunch," Rust says. "In some cases, getting more done faster with one machine may mean one machine can do the job of two."

The bottom line is, because of technological advances, farmers can be far more productive with much less work.

THE WORK OF A PASTOR

Technology also has transformed the work of a pastor in regard to studying the Bible and preparing his sermons. Before the industrial wave, very few copies of Scripture were available. What did exist were hand-copied bound volumes kept in libraries by the clergy. A new copy required many hours of tedious labor to reproduce the original exactly.

The invention of the printing press revolutionized not just the work of the pastor but the larger society as well. The first book off the new printing press was a Bible. Copies of the Scripture multiplied, as did copies of the concordance and thesaurus. These copies enabled more people to study the texts and the meanings of words.

The information age has accelerated the revolution beyond anything Johannes Gutenberg could have imagined when he published his first Bible in the fifteenth century. Now high-speed color presses can churn out Scripture portions at a rate that would make his head spin. Bible software allows a pastor or layman to instantly find a Bible reference or locate every use of a particular word or phrase in seconds, as well as dig into the underlying words. Sermon supports and worship resources are available on the internet, many of them for free.

As amazing as those advances are, and as much as an overworked pastor appreciates them, these new technologies have a definite downside.

In earlier ages, when copies of the Scripture were harder to come by, earnest believers memorized large portions of the Bible. Some of us had grandparents who could quote entire chapters of God's Word from memory—a feat most young people today would consider impossible, perhaps even a waste of time. The easy accessibility of published materials has engendered sloppy study habits and preparation without meditation. Many an overworked pastor is tempted to "google" his Sunday sermon, rather than fight for time to allow the Holy Spirit to guide him into God's message for the people. Doctrinal integrity can be eroded as sloppy sermons and lessons are posted on the internet for others to download and pass along.

THE POWER OF TECHNOLOGY

The Bible is talking about the power of new tools in Proverbs 14:4 where it says, "Where no oxen are, the crib is clean: but much increase is by the strength of the ox."

In other words, the ox was a *force multiplier*. When a farmer used an ox, much more work was done in far less time. The ox was "technology" at work, but the value of getting more done was offset by the "stuff in the stable" that had to be dealt with! Our goal as pastors is to take advantage of the technology "ox" to get more done while still keeping the stable "clean" of malodorous byproduct.

We can be helped in our vigilance by considering some questions suggested by Marshall McLuhan, author of *Understanding Media* and *The Global Village*, to evaluate the impact of technology.

Question one: *what does the medium (technology) enhance and extend?* This is an existing ability that is significantly improved by the aid of a tool. For instance, the automobile extends the range and speed of man.

Question two: *what does the medium obsolesce?* This is an old tool that is no longer useful because the new one provides such a great advantage. The automobile extends our speed of transportation, but it makes carriages and horses obsolete. The horse-drawn carriage doesn't totally disappear, but it is now primarily used for romance and entertainment—or seen in museums.

Question three: *what does the medium reverse into?* Technology will often reverse into some form of its opposite when it is overused. For example, when the car is overused or misused, it can actually result in traffic jams and even fatalities.[2]

Consider these questions in regard to printing technology. Before the printing press, few copies of books were available, especially to the common man. A single Bible might cost a year's wages. With the advent of the press, entire Bibles could be produced much more cheaply. Some elites in the Catholic church were frightened by the prospect of untrained commoners having access to the Bible. The printing press also put many manuscript copiers out of business. Before long, society saw that the printing press could be used for evil as well as good—propaganda, lies, and pornography began pouring off the press and into society.

So should the printing press have been outlawed because some misused it for sinful purposes? Of course not.

Consider the ox:

Benefits and Byproducts of Technology

	Increase of the Ox or Technology Benefits	Bad Byproducts
Ox	Less starvation/less work	"Stuff" in the stable, ox "maintenance"
Printing Press	Bibles for everybody	Wickedness and lies
Broadcast Media	Preaching the Gospel to masses, mass communication	Filthy communication
Internet	Increase of knowledge, communication, speed, and connectedness	Propagation of lies and pornography, gossip, and wasted time

Technology is not inherently evil. It is, however, a force multiplier with definite byproducts. As we've already noted, Paul was willing to use anything to reach more people, as long as its use did not violate a command of Scripture. And Jesus used what was available—fish, coins, object lessons, and stories—to enhance His message.

We should make godly use of the technology the Lord has made available to us. But we also should be keenly aware of the byproducts and keep our "stables" clean.

INDEPENDENT BAPTISTS AND TECHNOLOGY

Historically, independent Baptists were "early adopters" with regard to technology. I recently read about how J. Frank Norris used the new radio technology to get the Gospel out and drive traffic to their ministries. Many Christians at the time were upset at Norris for using the radio. The critics dismissed the new tool as "a toy, a fad that would not last. Why waste the Lord's money on such a foolish venture?"[3]

Our research revealed that healthy churches were much more likely to use the latest technologies for ministry purposes. In their outreach, healthy churches were much more likely to use every available medium to present the Gospel and project their ministry into surrounding communities:

Mailings (7 in 10)

Internet communication (10 in 10)

Newspaper ads (6 in 10)

Radio and TV (4 in 10)

Interestingly, there are some technologies that seem to have little if any bearing on health or growth. For example, the growing churches we studied were equally split on projection—half projected hymn lyrics on a screen, and half used hymnals alone.

From our visits to strong churches, we did notice they were more likely to implement a variety of technologies to help them do the work of the ministry more efficiently and effectively. Fundamentally, these churches didn't dismiss technology but rather carefully evaluated and

SPOTLIGHTING CHURCHES THAT WORK

COASTLINE BAPTIST CHURCH

OCEANSIDE, CALIFORNIA

While most of the healthy churches in our survey are using technology effectively, we asked Pastor Stephen Chappell to share what his church is doing, why, and how the Lord is blessing it. This is a snap-shot of one church and what's working well.

E-newsletter. This is sent once per month with teaser articles that link back to the church website. This newsletter is mailed to every email address in the membership and visitor database and is read by a large percentage of recipients. It helps the church see over 20,000 unique visits to their website each month.

Website videos and content. The church staff plans humorous videos or other content, and then they encourage the church family to share the website with friends, coworkers, and neighbors.

Screens and PowerPoint in services. The video projection screens are used for announcements, monthly update videos, sermon illustrations, and sermon outlines on Sunday mornings. Pastor Chappell shares, "You can use technology too much or in the wrong way. We are careful that it doesn't overpower the message, but in my experience, it helps to get and keep people's attention. People respond to this way of communicating. It's just where they are in this day and age."

Title slides for sermons. While he doesn't always use PowerPoint for his sermon outlines, he does always have a title slide with a graphic that illustrates the big idea behind his sermon. This causes the theme of the message to stick with people longer.

Short videos. The church staff will ocassionally produce a short video promoting a new sermon series, a new ministry opportunity, or an upcoming event. The church family responds well to this sort of communication.

COASTLINE BAPTIST CONTINUED...

Other ministry websites. The church has created a website for the music ministry, the adult class ministry, and the building program. These sites are regularly updated with information pertaining to those aspects of ministry.

Databases and church management systems. The office staff regularly employs and relies upon church management software for membership records, communication, giving records, visitor follow-up, ministry mailing lists, etc.

Twitter. The church recently began using a church account on twitter.com to post announcements, prayer requests, and pertinent information for members and those who wish to follow the ministry.

Sermon content posted online. Sunday's messages are posted, but the usage of those media files is interesting. "We're finding that most people click on a message and listen to or watch only the first five or ten minutes—most likely an effort to see what we're all about. Very few listen to the whole sermon." Literally, the church website has become a virtual visit!

In conclusion, Pastor Chappell shared these insightful thoughts: "Preaching against the technologies of culture, in my opinion, is sort of like preaching against the architectural style of someone's house. It's just where they live. And so, the modern technologies of culture are just where people live. We're certainly not selling out and going the wrong direction—we're simply using tools to get the attention of lost people and focus it on Christ. But we're using tools of communication that people identify with and understand.

"Honestly, we try to get ideas from a lot of other churches that are doing a good job in this area as well. We appreciate what we've learned from others, and we see God blessing that desire to learn and do better as a local church."

implemented it where it could be helpful in furthering the other work of the church.

Independent Baptists historically have used emerging technologies to reach more people. Today, however, it appears we are becoming more "risk averse" to new technologies because of the possible byproducts. *The trade off is that we are giving up potential for greater or more effective ministry by avoiding new technologies.* We will address this more in a coming chapter.

Other groups and denominations are successfully using the internet and other technologies to drive traffic and develop relationships. Yet, all the while many independent Baptists get farther and farther behind in our understanding of technology and the impact it is having on our communities. This ignorance has huge implications for our next generation of leaders who have grown up in a world where these technologies are pervasive.

For instance, it was recently reported that children between the ages of 10 and 16 are spending an average of 6 hours a day in front of a television or computer screen.[4] Some say the local church should have nothing to do with the internet, but consider the potential for influencing young lives if we leveraged the internet as an effective discipleship and mentoring tool for our churches! This is how the next generation is communicating, connecting, and building relationships.

Non-denominational churches are employing podcasting, social networking, email, texting, and every conceivable new communication tool to get their message out and to build relationships. They are harnessing the ox, while we are cursing it. The result is that our children, who are tuned toward those new technologies, find no wholesome connectedness between the technologies of life and the local church ministry.

No right-thinking pastor or parent believes it is good for children to be in front of a television or the internet for 6 hours each day, so we need to talk about managing the "ox" and cleaning up its byproducts with our children. But we also need to be greatly concerned with leveraging these technologies to reach out to our communities with the Gospel and information about our caring ministries.

INNOVATION OR EFFECTIVENESS?

A critical question to ask when evaluating technology is "why use it?" It seems many Christians and churches today are being led by culture rather than by the Holy Spirit. The contemporary church can't get enough of entertainment technologies, light shows, pop-music, and techno trends. The local church doesn't need to be "trendy" to reach people—it needs to be godly. Again, our goal is to duplicate the book of Acts.

Innovation merely for the sake of keeping up with culture is pointless. If our goal is constant reinvention and innovation, it's only a matter of time before technology takes the reigns and leads the local church down a slippery slope of compromise.

The goal is not innovation, but rather *effectiveness*. We must be compelled to communicate and to minister more effectively. And when the church is growing, the challenge is to minister to more people more effectively. We don't desire to use technology to be trendy—but we do desire to better speak the language of the people who use those technologies frequently.

This is where technology can make a wonderful difference. All of our communication and technology decisions should be focused on strengthening the message, improving the ministry, and helping people have clarity and understanding of God's truth.

Be careful about jumping on a technology bandwagon just because everyone else is doing it. But be careful about rejecting technological tools simply because someone else has misused them.

Healthy churches evaluate technology and tools in light of biblical fruit bearing. If a tool can help the church to bear more fruit, then it is employed for God's glory.

The ox is powerful and dangerous. Its byproducts are nasty. But the ox is worth having if we keep our stables clean and the ox under control. God forbid we preach against the ox because of the stuff on the stable floor. Let's take hold of any technology that is not a silly fad and harness it for the glory of God!

We've journeyed from stranger, to first-time guest, to new Christian, to new member—and we've discussed in this chapter that effective tools and technology can support all of the practices of healthy churches. Now it's time to press forward into spiritual maturity. Healthy churches continue the work of spiritual growth. Let's find out how.

CHAPTER NINE
TAKE–AWAYS

- Tools and technology can increase our ability to reap a greater harvest.

- Healthy churches employ tools and technologies to help them perform the other six practices more effectively.

- Healthy churches evaluate technology and implement it when it can further God's work.

- We risk losing our next generation of leaders if we are averse to new technologies and tools.

- We don't need to be trendy to reach people.

- The goal is not innovation but effectiveness.

- Our technology decisions should be focused on strengthening the message and improving the ministry.

COMPEL SPIRITUAL COMMITMENTS

*"As ye know how we exhorted and comforted and charged
every one of you, as a father doth his children, That ye
would walk worthy of God, who hath called you unto his
kingdom and glory."*—1 THESSALONIANS 2:11–12

There is a vast difference between a casual attendee and a committed Christian. Churches all across the nation have "casual attendees." In fact, the contemporary church has mastered the art of casual Christianity—a "have it your way" brand of self-centered Christianity. They teach distorted definitions of "radical grace" and extreme forms of "liberty" in which seemingly "anything goes." The non-committal, all-tolerant, social gospel of "many ways to Heaven" is prevalent in our society.

Biblical, local church ministry is altogether different. Jesus said in Matthew 28:18–20, "…All power is given unto me in heaven and in earth. Go ye therefore, and teach all nations, baptizing them in the name of the Father, and of the Son, and of the Holy Ghost: Teaching them to observe all things whatsoever I have commanded you: and, lo, I am with you alway, even unto the end of the world. Amen."

Of His followers Jesus said, "So likewise, whosoever he be of you that forsaketh not all that he hath, he cannot be my disciple" (Luke 14:33). And again in Luke 14:26–27 He said, "If any man come to me, and hate not his father, and mother, and wife, and children, and brethren, and sisters, yea, and his own life also, he cannot be my disciple. And whosoever doth not bear his cross, and come after me, cannot be my disciple."

Let's face it—this is tough stuff to swallow for an unbeliever. In fact, those who heard Jesus often responded in this way, "Many therefore of his disciples, when they had heard this, said, This is an hard saying; who can hear it?" (John 6:60).

Our charge is to lead men to Christ and ultimately to complete self abandonment for the eternal purpose of His will. There is no way to accomplish this task tentatively or hesitantly. Timid, passive, fearful spiritual leadership never developed passionate, fully-committed disciples of Jesus Christ.

In the next chapter we're going to take a closer look at personal discipleship—moving a believer from salvation to fruitbearing. But without the quality that we will visit in this chapter, real discipleship is impossible.

In all of our research, this quality or character trait was present in every healthy church. For instance, in the survey, healthy churches were more likely to have invitations and to use response cards with their congregation. This is the courageous, biblical quality of compelling God's people to make spiritual commitments. Healthy churches are courageous to lovingly but purposefully nudge people forward spiritually—for their own benefit. This is the opposite of passivity. It is active, it is biblical, and it is unapologetic. This kind of leadership is patient and compassionate, but nonetheless focused and directional.

THE PATTERN OF THE NEW TESTAMENT

We see this characteristic of compelling spiritual commitments first in the ministry of Jesus. Think of the unwavering call of Christ upon the lives of His disciples— "And he saith unto them, Follow me, and I will make you fishers of men" (Matthew 4:19). "But Jesus said unto him, Follow me; and let the dead bury their dead" (Matthew 8:22). There was no room for negotiation. His call was resolute. There was no ambiguity or ambivalence. He was not vague or hesitant. He was unequivocal, leaving no room for doubt, uncertainty, or indecision.

We see the same in Mark chapter 10 as a rich young ruler comes to Jesus desiring a casual brand of follower-ship: "And when he was gone forth into the way, there came one running, and kneeled to him, and asked him, Good Master, what shall I do that I may inherit eternal life? And Jesus said unto him, Why callest thou me good? there is none good but one, that is, God. Thou knowest the commandments, Do not commit adultery, Do not kill, Do not steal, Do not bear false witness, Defraud not, Honour thy father and mother. And he answered and said unto him, Master, all these have I observed from my youth. Then Jesus beholding him loved him, and said unto him, One thing thou lackest: go thy way, sell whatsoever thou hast, and give to the poor, and thou shalt have treasure in heaven: and come, take up the cross, and follow me. And he was sad at that saying, and went away grieved: for he had great possessions" (Mark 10:17–22).

Jesus actually let this man, who would not admit his sin, walk away. He was not caustic to this man—He didn't drive Him off; but rather He presented a choice, compelled a decision, and then let the man exercise his free will.

We see the same pattern in the ministry of the Apostle Paul. Notice how Paul compelled his converts in 1 Thessalonians 2:11–12, "As ye know how we exhorted and comforted and charged every one of you, as a father doth his children, That ye would walk worthy of God, who hath called you unto his kingdom and glory." He commanded young Timothy to "Preach the word; be instant in season, out of season; reprove, rebuke, exhort with all longsuffering and doctrine" (2 Timothy 4:2).

Throughout all of Scripture, it is the practice of God, and men on a mission from God, to compel people to adopt positions of surrender, obedience, commitment, and self abandonment. And such is the practice of growing local churches. While they demonstrate a spirit of patience as all believers "grow in grace" (2 Peter 3:18), they nonetheless, compel that growth forward by urging Christians to courageously and obediently go to the next level of faith and surrender.

This is a decision on the part of the pastor to embrace this somewhat uncomfortable mantle of leadership. Some people resent being biblically compelled. They will not appreciate being provoked unto love and good works. (Hebrews 10:24, "And let us consider one another to provoke unto love and to good works.") Some will look for more ambiguous, passive, and non-assertive leadership. But healthy churches do not attempt to avoid biblical commitment for the sake of pleasing the masses. They stand with Christ—creating watershed decision points and compelling biblical life-change.

UNDERSTAND THE SPIRIT

For the sake of clarity, let us articulate what we are not suggesting. This kind of spiritual leadership is not caustic, intimidating, or arrogant. It is not brow-beating, guilt-tripping, or manipulating. For there is plenty of this sort of man-made, carnal approach to ministry. We are not advocating overbearing spiritual authority, spiritual abuse, or the use of a bully-pulpit.

Rather, this is meek, humble, Christ-centered spiritual leadership simply standing on the authority of the Word of God and calling God's people to obey Him. This is to be in the spirit of 2 Timothy 2:25, "In meekness instructing those that oppose themselves…." It involves leading by example, while simultaneously challenging those who follow.

Do you ever feel "bad" asking people to do what God instructs? Do you shirk away from preaching or teaching on giving? Do you soften God's message of surrender and sacrificial living? Do you hesitate to lead people into the realm of faith and obedience? Think about it. Who stands to gain when we compel people to honor God? *They* do!

How desperately we need leadership and local churches that will call people away from spiritual indecision and vacillation; and call them to courageous, confident Christian obedience. When we fail to compel people forward, we cause them to miss the blessing of the sanctified life. When we fear the risk of losing them, we condemn them to spiritual infancy.

Yes, there is risk, but it is the same biblical kind of risk that Jesus and the apostles took in developing their disciples. Churches across our nation are afraid to take this kind of bold approach to spiritual leadership and biblical Christianity.

This attribute of compelling spiritual commitments begins with a courageous spirit, but also involves a strategy. Once you have chosen to step into this role of tender strength and gentle firmness, you must define biblically the commitments that you will compel people to make. And the Bible has already done this for us.

DEFINE THE DIRECTION

Some of the decisions that healthy local churches compel people toward have already been mentioned in previous chapters. But for the sake of the big picture, this list comprises some of the basic biblical decisions we should actively encourage people to make.

1. Compel people to trust Christ. Through soulwinning, follow-up, and personal relationships we should continually compel the lost to the Saviour.

2. Compel people to be baptized. This is the first thing that believers in the book of Acts did—in obedience to Christ's example and command. Teach new Christians the importance of obedience to Christ and of public identification with Him in the church.

3. Compel people to faithful church attendance. God desires for His people to assemble to worship Him and to hear His Word. Teach new Christians that this step of commitment is essential to their spiritual growth.

4. Compel people to enroll in an adult class. For the last two generations we independent Baptists have organized our churches through the Sunday school. Though many churches have gone the "small-group" route for home study, our experience still points to strong

HERITAGE BAPTIST CHURCH

SAN LEANDRO, CALIFORNIA

In San Leandro, California (near Oakland), God is mightily at work through the ministry of the Heritage Baptist Church—a church plant that began January 1999. At that time, Alan Fong was a businessman who helped to start the church with thirty original members. Over two years of ministry, God began to work in Alan's heart about pastoring. He became the pastor in July of 2004 when the founding pastor returned to the mission field. By that time the church had grown to 250 weekly attendees.

Since that time, Heritage has grown to a weekly attendance of 450 people—reaching a high percentage of professionals in the San Francisco Bay Area and establishing a ministry on the high profile college campus of Cal Berkeley. The focus of the ministry has been soulwinning and discipleship—reaching the lost and compelling new Christians to make spiritual commitments.

Pastor Fong shared, "We live in a day when people are afraid of commitment. They don't see it at home or in the workplace, and so they fear it. We find that we literally have to take people by the hand and lead them into spiritual commitments, showing them that it's better than they think it is."

When asked about what commitments they are leading new Christians toward, he shared three: First, enroll in a small discipleship class. "My wife conducts one for ladies and I conduct one for men. This small class offers our new Christians a chance to ask any question, and this allows us to minister 'up close' in their lives. We find that we can see them grow more rapidly if they will make this first commitment to a small discipleship setting."

Second, attend services on a regular basis. "People are much more responsive to the preaching if they are also being discipled one on one. Our disciples are always the first to respond to the invitations. The third commitment is simply following in believer's baptism.

HERITAGE BAPTIST CONTINUED...

When asked about the different pace of growth among different Christians, Pastor Fong shared these thoughts: "We keep encouraging people to grow in grace, no matter where they are. Often I will ask a Christian what questions he might have. Sometimes it's about the growth of a spouse. Other times it may be a job schedule or a commute that is hindering someone from taking the next step. We try to discern the greatest level of commitment new Christians should have considering his spiritual maturity and availability. We try to be sensitive to those factors."

While God always uses the preaching of His Word to compel spiritual growth, Pastor Fong felt that God has also greatly blessed the one-on-one efforts of talking with people, praying with them, and encouraging them forward spiritually.

He shared, "I am a high-touch pastor. I like to be involved personally in the lives of our church family and to know how they are and in what direction they are headed. Every week I write many letters, personal emails, and make many personal contacts. At least fifty times a week I will call individuals in our church family—including deacons and staff—just to see how they are doing and to let them know I prayed for them. God uses that to help people keep going forward spiritually.

When asked about the risks involved, Pastor Fong said he fears that people will comply with the forward step, but inwardly still fear following through—such as tithing, etc. "It's often these people that will start to falter in their Christian lives because they took a step forward and then struggled with that step. In those cases we try to be sensitive and caring. There are times when someone just isn't ready to make a commitment, in which case we back off a little bit and give him some room to grow, but we keep encouraging and loving him."

The health and growth at Heritage Baptist Church is a tremendous indicator that people need spiritual leadership to compel them forward. Pastor Fong's final advice: "The pastor has to keep stirring up the fires of commitment, even with those who are strong and growing—the pastor's job of stoking the coals is never over!"

Sunday schools as being more effective in connecting more people to regular teaching and fellowship. We have found that more people will participate in an adult class on Sunday morning than in a small group on a weeknight (74% of all independent Baptist church members attend Sunday school).

5. Compel people to join the church. Explain to prospective members and new members that there is a level of commitment involved with being a faithful member of the local church. Don't be afraid to state: "Being a member of a local church is a biblical commitment to a body of believers, a body of doctrine, and the body of Christ."

Ephesians 2:19 states, "Now therefore ye are no more strangers and foreigners, but fellowcitizens with the saints, and of the household of God."

6. Compel people to participate in new members classes and personal discipleship. In our survey, healthy churches (70% of them) offered a new members class and some sort of midweek discipleship or study program. (We will share more of this concept in the next chapter.)

One of the primary ways we (at Lancaster Baptist) enlist people to the purpose and process of our church is through our development of new members. Presently we host a four-week new members' class which prospective members are welcome to attend as well. This is specifically held to build the core of our church family—to compel them to make spiritual commitments.

In this class we teach them who we are, where we are going, and how God intends to lead us there. We teach the biblical purposes of our church—loving God, growing together, and serving others.

During these four weeks of lessons, I (PWC) teach on doctrine, Baptist distinctives, ministry philosophy (such as music and principles of biblical separation), and discipleship. I share with them how this local church desires to support and develop their faith. I introduce them to the soulwinning ministries, adult classes, youth ministry, church staff, etc.

This is a critical time of compelling spiritual commitments. I presume that they are attending because God led them, and I clearly spell out what we believe is God's biblical agenda for their lives. And they appreciate it. In fact, they really get excited and motivated about their spiritual growth.

7. Compel people to obey God. We continually challenge our church family in loving, worshipping, giving, serving, soulwinning, and faithfulness. As you prepare Bible messages, remember that your messages should lead people to a biblical precipice of decision. From there they will exercise their free will. Many will step out in faith and honor God—and benefit from His blessings. Many will hesitate and pause spiritually. They may still love you and still grow at their own pace—so don't stop compelling, but don't get impatient with those who don't grow as fast as you would prefer.

RADICAL SPIRITUAL GROWTH

Radical spiritual growth happens when people make radical spiritual commitments. We already know this, but actually leading people into this realm can be fearful and seem risky.

This type of growth happens when a pastor's passionate pursuit of God's vision compels others to that vision as well. This vision must be biblical, and the fulfillment or pursuit of it must be an act of obedience to God. But healthy churches have a pastor who is committed to God's vision and to challenging people to own that vision.

As you seek to be a "compelling" leader, you will find that there are three types of responses from the church family:

1. *Those who will gladly benefit from the vision*
2. *Those who will comfortably contribute to the vision*
3. *Those who will give their lives to the vision*

Not everybody will make every spiritual commitment that you compel them toward, but don't ever stop pursuing the vision of God. This passion will cause many in your church family to participate in spiritual growth and ministry at a level they would have never known.

Nehemiah 2:18 explains how Nehemiah shared God's vision and the people embraced it. "Then I told them of the hand of my God which was good upon me; as also the king's words that he had spoken unto me. And they said, Let us rise up and build. So they strengthened their hands for this good work." The leader said, "This is what God wants us to do," and the people said, "Then let's get it done."

Think of the passion that the Apostle Paul had for the Galatian Christians when he wrote in Galatians 4:19, "My little children, of whom I travail in birth again until Christ be formed in you." He unashamedly compelled them to return to the pure faith of the Gospel, and he called them forward in spiritual transformation.

In healthy churches, the pastor courageously leads the way, and the people share the purpose. They know what they believe, and they understand the process of compelling spiritual commitments. If the pastor, by God's grace, will develop a loving spirit of forward momentum, he is setting the stage for reproducing devoted disciples of the Lord Jesus Christ.

CHAPTER TEN
TAKE–AWAYS

- Christ desires to have an exclusive, committed relationship with His own.

- Healthy churches are courageous to compel people forward to spiritual maturity.

- The New Testament pattern shows Christ and the apostles compelling Christians to greater commitment.

- Our compelling must flow from humble hearts and compassionate leadership—not guilt or manipulation.

- We must define the "next steps" and compel believers to take them.

- Radical spiritual growth is the product of radical commitment.

- Not everybody will make the commitments we compel— we must love them where they are.

- Healthy churches are not afraid to ask people to take the next step in their spiritual lives.

DEVELOP DEVOTED DISCIPLES

"And the things that thou hast heard of me among many
witnesses, the same commit thou to faithful men, who
shall be able to teach others also."—2 TIMOTHY 2:2

The first time I (PWC) ever saw personal, vital, one-on-one discipleship happening was on a visit to the mission field. After a long flight to the Philippines, I was jet-lagged and preparing to preach in Cebu City with Missionary John Honeycutt.

That afternoon, before church, John pulled me aside into a building and said, "I'd like to show you how we are preparing the future church planters." We then entered a classroom where there were about fifteen young Filipino Christians who were sitting at tables with mature Christians and being trained and taught in a one-on-one setting. They were being led through a carefully prepared curriculum that not only grounded them in Bible doctrine and scriptural foundations, it also trained them simultaneously in how to disciple others.

In fact, each of the Christians being discipled was actually required to take one new convert through the same discipleship curriculum. This group of disciples was to be the hub of the next new church that this missionary was intending to plant.

In that moment, my feelings of jet lag gave way to an eye opening and life changing ministry moment. I had never seen such deliberate and methodical discipleship. The sight and the philosophy resonated in my heart, and the Holy Spirit seemed to say, "Why not at your church? Why not in America?" It was in that moment that God implanted a strong desire to take this practice back to my local church and to other local churches in our nation.

To many independent Baptists, leading dynamic soulwinning churches that are *also* dynamic discipleship churches has been a bit elusive. In fact, I remember a day not so long ago, when among vibrant soulwinning churches, the term "discipleship" was viewed with negative connotations. Personal discipleship is in no way detrimental to personal soulwinning. The two are not mutually incompatible. This it not an "either/or" proposition.

Not only can fervent soulwinning and focused discipleship co-exist—they should *complement* each other with a great multiplying effect. In our research, healthy churches were nearly three times more likely than struggling churches to provide a personal discipleship program.

In our survey, healthy churches were much more likely to have a separate program for discipleship rather than integrating it into other ministries or programs of the church. They were also much more likely to have regular times of prayer as a church family.

Healthy churches keep people and lead them into spiritual maturity. They learn how to nurture people to the point where they desire to stay and to serve. They labor to ground people in the faith of Christ. Colossians 2:7 states the Lord's desire for His people to be "rooted and built up in him, and stablished in the faith, as ye have been taught, abounding therein with thanksgiving." God is first interested in church health and then church growth. He is interested in healthy growth, and He blesses the churches that focus on developing devoted disciples. Consider three principles:

First, discipleship is scriptural—2 Timothy 2:1–4, "Thou therefore, my son, be strong in the grace that is in Christ Jesus. And the things that thou hast heard of me among many witnesses, the same commit thou to faithful men, who shall be able to teach others also. Thou therefore endure hardness, as a good soldier of Jesus Christ. No man that warreth entangleth himself with the affairs of this life; that he may please him who hath chosen him to be a soldier." Acts 2:42 states, "And they continued steadfastly…." God is an advocate of fruit that remains.

Second, discipleship is personal—Galatians 4:19, "My little children, of whom I travail in birth again until Christ be formed in you."

Third, discipleship is patient—First Peter 2:2, "As newborn babes, desire the sincere milk of the word, that ye may grow thereby." Second Peter 3:18, "But grow in grace, and in the knowledge of our Lord and Saviour Jesus Christ. To him be glory both now and for ever. Amen."

It should be our desire to keep people in the local church—not for selfish motives, but for the pure motive of grounding them in the faith of Jesus Christ. And keeping people in the local church is primarily about how we disciple them and care spiritually for them.

I (pwc) have heard pastors joke about "back-door revivals." Sometimes their spirits are cynical and calloused, and they refer to people leaving the church as though leaving is a good thing. Yet, when we entered the Gospel ministry none of us enlisted for the cause of "back-door revival." This is not what we had in mind when we began laboring for the local church.

While I understand that Christ will purge His church and at times people will leave the church for a variety of reasons, our goal should never be to lose people. Let's examine what it takes to establish people in the faith and to "close the back door."

UNDERSTAND GOD'S OWNERSHIP OF HIS CHURCH

At times we see a cycle of Christians being truly faithful in service and sacrifice. Some become actively involved for a season and then fall away. But this cycle is not God's intent, and we cannot minister with the assumption that this cycle is "normal." It may be common, but it should not be normal.

By faith, we should believe that God can strengthen, settle, and keep those that come to Him. First Peter 5:10 explains, "But the God of all grace, who hath called us unto his eternal glory by Christ Jesus, after that ye have suffered a while, make you perfect, stablish, strengthen, settle you." It is the heart and intent of God that His people would be faithful until death—pressing toward the mark steadfastly, unmoved, and unwavering. First Corinthians 15:58 states it this way, "Therefore, my beloved brethren, be ye stedfast, unmoveable, always abounding in the work of the Lord, forasmuch as ye know that your labour is not in vain in the Lord."

With this goal in mind, we must be aware of the following principles as we disciple and develop our church family:

God is sovereign in the affairs of His church.

"Man proposes, but God disposes." This is the church of Jesus Christ, and He will add to it and remove from it. We must recognize and constantly be mindful of His sovereignty and ownership.

It is not our job to trap people into being discipled or staying faithful.

The Holy Spirit will do much better than we will! We don't need "Ten Ways to Guilt-trip People into Staying." Many times our efforts tend toward manipulating people to do the things we want them to do. We attempt to manufacture commitment and performance.

We can't "hold the church together" on our own—it frustrates people, and it is impossible to try to micromanage the church family at that level. The commitment of our church family should be a Holy Spirit generated commitment that flows from genuine hearts.

Churches that use guilt or manipulation to keep people will develop a toxicity that is detrimental to spiritual health and growth.

An atmosphere where questioning authority is akin to questioning God leads to an obscured reality. It is far better to teach people to walk with

God individually and to discern His voice for themselves, while at the same time encouraging biblical practices of accountability to spiritual leaders.

We must remember that the pastor or staff is not the glue that "holds it all together"—the Holy Spirit is.

FOCUS ON PERSONAL DISCIPLESHIP

How can we engage new converts in spiritual growth? What process and efforts should a local church put in place to help people become the strong Christians that God intends? I (PWC) believe there are several pillars of discipleship that God blesses in local church life. These are four primary efforts at Lancaster Baptist Church that God has used to disciple and ground those that come to Jesus Christ. They are as follows:

1. *The preaching and teaching of biblical messages*
2. *The intentional development of new members*
3. *The ministry of effective adult classes*
4. *The training of Christians through one-on-one discipleship*

Let's take a closer look at these four elements:

The preaching and teaching of biblical messages
What we "win" them with is the same thing we "keep" them with—and that must be the Word of God. While many churches today are attempting to draw and keep people with entertainment, trendy methods, and pop-psychology, may we reach and keep them with the solid substance of Scripture. The very baseline of winning people *to* God and keeping them *with* God is the Word of God. I (PWC) have never been a proponent of winning or keeping people through hype, guilt, or gifts.

As we stated earlier, plan message series that will deeply ground your church family and mature their faith in Christ. God still uses the preaching and teaching of His Word—and we are called to do both.

It is possible to stay on the surface of topical preaching and to preach those topics that most resonate with your personality. It is another thing altogether to be a minister of the whole counsel of God. This commitment to preaching is what develops a biblically orientated church family. It is the Word of God that effectually works in hearts (1 Thessalonians 2:13).

In addition to biblical preaching, we must challenge Christians to value the services of the church. God does. Hebrews 10:25 says, "Not forsaking the assembling of ourselves together, as the manner of some is; but exhorting one another: and so much the more, as ye see the day approaching." A phrase that every church member is familiar with at Lancaster Baptist Church is "three to thrive—Sunday morning, Sunday night, and Wednesday night!"

The intentional development of new members

We visited this in the last chapter. Healthy churches act quickly to orientate new members in their doctrine, philosophy of ministry, biblical purpose, and the flow of ministry at the local church.

At Lancaster Baptist, we've stated our purpose this way: Loving God, Growing Together, and Serving Others. And this purpose is explained with the following terms and Scriptures:

Loving God—Mark 12:30, "And thou shalt love the Lord thy God with all thy heart, and with all thy soul, and with all thy mind, and with all thy strength: this is the first commandment." This is about participating in worship services, coming to more than one service a week, responding to the preaching, giving to and honoring the Lord, and conforming our lives to the image of Christ.

Growing together—Acts 2:42, "And they continued stedfastly in the apostles' doctrine and fellowship, and in breaking of bread, and in prayers." This is when we encourage new members to attend an adult class, complete one-on-one discipleship, develop a daily walk, and participate in the *Wednesdays in the Word* weekly Bible study.

Serving others—First Peter 4:10, "As every man hath received the gift, even so minister the same one to another, as good stewards of the manifold grace of God." God desires for every Christian to find a place of service in the local body. He also commands us to reach out to friends and neighbors and bring them to Christ.

As a side note on developing new members, a major mistake we often make in local church ministry is that we don't allow time for growth in regards to biblical convictions and separation. There are some things that should be emphasized immediately to new Christians and new members, but there are other practical things that are "better felt than telt." This happens when those in positions of leadership consistently model biblical standards of separation.

For example, the Bible does indicate that there is a difference between a strong Christian and a weak Christian (Romans 14 and 15, Galatians 5:13). Strong Christians must "bear the infirmities of the weak" and be willing to nurture them to spiritual strength. Stronger Christians will embrace the responsibilities of influence and not cause another brother to stumble. It takes much time and travail (Galatians 4:19) to disciple and mentor a weaker or younger Christian in the practice of a holy lifestyle. The best way to do this is by the example of strong Christians first exemplifying a holy lifestyle and then mentoring someone one on one toward that lifestyle (see Titus 2:1–8). We are to show a pattern of good works and then teach that pattern.

The ministry of effective adult classes

A third avenue of personal discipleship that is extremely effective in healthy churches is the adult Bible class ministry. These classes provide biblical lessons, intentional fellowship, connection, care, and accountability. They provide smaller group settings where relationships can develop among those of similar life stages.

Many years ago we made a philosophical decision at Lancaster Baptist—to make the adult class ministry the hub of personal discipleship, soulwinning, and relationship development. Every attempt is made to invite and enroll first-time guests into an adult class. Nearly all activity, follow-up, discipleship, fellowship, and friendships are developed in connection with an adult class. The most important benefit each class provides is focused Bible teaching.

Over the years, whenever we have hit a wall of growth or organization, we looked to the development of the adult classes first. We have added classes, divided age groups, enlisted more teachers, and expanded their role. This ongoing organizational effort has helped our church to grow spiritually and numerically.

The training of Christians through one-on-one discipleship

An effective one-on-one discipleship ministry seeks to enlist every new believer into a curriculum of spiritual development.

When Jesus began His ministry on earth, He did not start at the organizational level. He could have come to the existing organizations of the faithful in His day and said, "O gentlemen, I'm here, I'm in charge, and this is the way we will change things!" Instead, Jesus chose to take the approach of a servant leader and quietly influence the lives of a small group of men whom He then entrusted and empowered to impact the world.

There is something very effective and powerful about this kind of one-on-one mentoring. Logistically, it requires great effort to put into place, but the fruit is worth all of the effort. This ministry requires choosing a solid teaching. (For discipleship teaching ideas see: *Daily in the Word, Third Edition*, by John Honeycutt, available through www.strivingtogether.com.) It also involves choosing faithful and strong Christians who may be able to "teach others also" (2 Timothy 2:2). Those Christians need to be trained and taught how to disciple and mentor others. Additionally, this discipleship ministry needs a time and a place and a voice—a way to enlist and involve new believers in the process.

At Lancaster Baptist, the one-on-one discipleship takes place every Wednesday night in a room set up with refreshments and small tables where two or four can sit and work through a one-hour discipleship lesson. Every new Christian and new member is encouraged to participate in this ministry. The curriculum includes ten lessons through which a new Christian may work at his own pace. The meeting time provides a private setting where new Christians can ask any question or raise any concern.

Upon completion, the new Christians are given a certificate during the Wednesday night Bible study in the main auditorium, where they are welcomed into the main service at that point. By this time, they've already developed a habit of coming on Wednesday nights as well.

As a final note on personal discipleship, it is vital that you emphasize the ministry of the Holy Spirit. The Christian life is a linkage to the omnipotent resources of God. Our lists of rules, our management skills, and our most cleverly devised strategies are no replacement for teaching people to abide

SPOTLIGHTING CHURCHES THAT WORK

SPOTLIGHTING CHURCHES THAT WORK

VICTORY BAPTIST CHURCH

NORTH HOLLYWOOD, CALIFORNIA

For Pastor Rob Badger of Victory Baptist Church, discipleship is not a ministry of the church, but rather the focus of it—from salvation to spiritual maturity. His goal was not to have a big church in three years, but rather a strong church in ten years.

Pastor Badger began planting Victory Baptist Church during his senior year of Bible college—September 2004. The church was being planted by Lancaster Baptist, and Rob was driving down to North Hollywood each weekend with a team of church members and students to knock on doors and conduct services.

In June of 2005, Rob, his wife Tina, and their small children moved to North Hollywood to pastor full time. Thirty-five other churches helped support the Badgers as they began.

At this same time, Missionary John Honeycutt spent three weeks with the Badgers training them in the use of the *Daily in the Word* discipleship curriculum. They mapped the city, knocked on every door, and invited the people to three special nights of Bible study. This was done three weeks in a row and introduced the Badgers to the people who would come to Christ and eventually become the core members of Victory Baptist.

From day one, the Badgers have viewed all of their church planting efforts through the lens of discipleship. As they continually knock on doors and share the Gospel, they are seeking opportunities to sit down with people and work through the *Daily in the Word* discipleship materials one on one. At one point, early in the church life, the Badgers had fifteen different people they were meeting with on a weekly basis—people they had met while going door to door.

In Rob's words, "When discipling new Christians, you are insuring that they don't merely develop outward standards. Early in our ministry, we saw people come into the church and quickly appear to adopt our standards for the sake of fitting in. Our discipleship efforts have helped Christians get the Word of God into their hearts

VICTORY BAPTIST CONTINUED...

first, and then change happens from the inside out—the way the Christian life is supposed to work."

When asked for his advice to pastors seeking to develop a better approach to discipleship, he said, "Don't be afraid to think outside of the box. At first we struggled with how to structure our Wednesday night service. We wanted it to be the hub of our discipleship program, but we weren't sure how. We tried a lot of things that didn't work—like discipling the whole group, or allowing fairly young Christians to start discipling others a bit too soon. But we weren't afraid to try, and some things we tried worked very well."

The Badgers minister in a pagan culture with much cultism and deception. Many of the people they are reaching have never even held a Bible, much less read it. So their approach has been very foundational and elemental—building precept upon precept. Pastor Badger never makes a personal visit or responds to a need without taking a discipleship lesson along with him—hoping that he can sit down and work through a lesson with the person he is meeting. (The first lesson is always on salvation!)

When asked what has worked well, Rob said, "Using our Wednesday night service to teach the Bible systematically has been very blessed. We've taught our church family through *First Steps for New Christians*, *Daily in the Word*, and now we're working through major Bible doctrines. We've had to be creative with our schedule and format, but God is blessing the emphasis on His Word."

In addition to Sunday services, Pastor Badger focuses on one-on-one discipleship for new Christians and teaching the Bible (and allowing questions) to the group on Wednesday nights. The people the Badgers originally discipled in their first year are now serving and leading in ministries and helping others to grow as well.

In his words, "One-on-one discipleship is amazing! It is absolutely the way to go! We are now discipling our teens one on one before church on Sunday nights."

After nearly four years, the church is consistently averaging 125 in attendance. And it is obvious that developing devoted disciples permeates every aspect in the weekly life of this local church.

in Jesus Christ and to be led by His Spirit in their daily lives. The process of discipleship cannot be contained in a ten-week curriculum. It is a life-long process. Galatians 5:16–17 admonishes, "This I say then, Walk in the Spirit, and ye shall not fulfil the lust of the flesh. For the flesh lusteth against the Spirit, and the Spirit against the flesh: and these are contrary the one to the other: so that ye cannot do the things that ye would."

The primary methods of developing devoted disciples are these:

1. *The preaching and teaching of biblical messages*
2. *The intentional development of new members*
3. *The ministry of effective adult classes*
4. *The training of Christians through one-on-one discipleship*

PRACTICE PASTORAL LOVE AND OVERSIGHT

There is one more area of "keeping Christians faithful" that I (pwc) would like to visit as we conclude this chapter. Everything we've talked about to this point is about grounding people in God's Word—this is primary. Secondary to this would be the spiritual care and oversight provided by the pastor and spiritual care-givers in the church family.

In other words, people don't always fall away from faithfulness because they weren't grounded. Sometimes they leave for reasons of personal conflict, strained relationships, offense, or hurt. If someone is offended at our doctrine or biblical practice, we most likely won't be able to retain them. Yet, in my experience, most people who "leave church" intentionally, leave for reasons that could have been resolved with the right pastoral love, oversight, and intervention.

It's hard to disciple people that aren't attending. Therefore, it behooves us to be peacemakers and to lovingly and graciously intervene to resolve problems and restore relationships in the body that the Word of God might continue to have its effect in hearts.

Acts 20:28–30 says, "Take heed therefore unto yourselves, and to all the flock, over the which the Holy Ghost hath made you overseers, to feed the church of God, which he hath purchased with his own blood.

For I know this, that after my departing shall grievous wolves enter in among you, not sparing the flock. Also of your own selves shall men arise, speaking perverse things, to draw away disciples after them."

Healthy churches have vigilant under-shepherds who labor and pray for the protection and health of the whole flock. Consider these practices as you strive to provide loving, pastoral oversight.

Confront the problems in the flock.

Every church has misunderstandings and issues, because every church has people! Be willing to go to the problems, and try to resolve them with biblical humility and compassion. Problems usually don't just "go away"—they grow. So, learn how to put fires out while they are still small. Some days you may feel as though you have done nothing but put out fires—but if the Word of God and the Holy Spirit has a more free course in your church, your time has been well spent.

In my book *The Spiritual Leader* I referenced that churches sometimes attract pathological antagonists—scorners who are compelled to find or invent problems. These people cannot always be helped, but you should make every effort to help them through God's grace and to protect others from being hurt by them.

In Philippians 4:2 Paul writes, "I beseech Euodias, and beseech Syntyche, that they be of the same mind in the Lord."

Lovingly encourage the flock.

Give your best energy and efforts to fanning the flames of growth in godliness in the lives of people who have tender hearts. This encouragement is positive, proactive, communicative, and edifying. It may be through emails, text messages, personal letters, phone calls, visits, and personal prayer times. Do everything the Holy Spirit prompts you to do in regards to encouraging people.

One leader said it this way: "Be better at growing grass than killing weeds." Be better at encouraging a positive spirit than dealing with the bad ones. As a pastor and staff, be active in doing little things that encourage the church family. Deliver a gift, visit those with trials, reach out to those who are hurting. Open your home and your heart in Christ-like hospitality.

How many personal notes or emails have the members of your church family received from you in the past two weeks?

Consistently pray for the flock.

The battle for a healthy church family is spiritual and must be fought on our knees. Ephesians 6:12 states, "For we wrestle not against flesh and blood, but against principalities, against powers, against the rulers of the darkness of this world, against spiritual wickedness in high places."

Ultimately the battle is the Lord's. The local church belongs to Jesus Christ, and no one loves it more than He does. Yet, as His appointed overseers, may we do everything within our power to develop devoted disciples of Jesus Christ. This is His purpose for the church.

CHAPTER ELEVEN
TAKE–AWAYS

- Healthy churches understand the value of one-on-one discipleship.

- Discipleship is scriptural, personal, and patient.

- God is sovereign, and we cannot trap people into staying faithful to God.

- Four primary avenues of spiritual discipleship in healthy churches are these:

  1. *The preaching and teaching of biblical messages*
  2. *The intentional development of new members*
  3. *The ministry of effective adult classes*
  4. *The training of Christians through one-on-one discipleship*

- Discipleship must emphasize the ministry and leadership of the Holy Spirit.

- People often leave a church for reasons that could have been resolved.

- Healthy churches have pastors that help resolve relational conflicts in the church family.

PART THREE

STRIVING TOGETHER
FOR THE FAITH

In part one we studied the history and present state of our "band of brothers"—the independent Baptist churches of our nation. We were challenged to consider the fruit factors and the natural dynamics that impact our harvest. We were also greatly encouraged with the fact that independent Baptist churches across America are growing and going forward.

In part two we studied positive deviance—the seven practices of healthy local churches. These seven traits were abundantly present in the healthiest churches surveyed, and woefully lacking in the most struggling churches surveyed. Perhaps the study of those seven practices encouraged and challenged you as it did us! While we are doing many things well in our local churches, there is much room for improvement and growth in these seven biblical practices.

As we turn the page to part three we would like to ask this question— what is the potential? What are the implications of pressing forward with great faith, striving together, encouraging one another, and laboring together to plant new churches? If we could, once again, be soldiers fighting the same battle and pursuing the same biblical dream, what might God do through us?

Together, we stand before a great open door! But there are also many adversaries, as Paul stated in 1 Corinthians 16:9, "For a great door and effectual is opened unto me, and there are many adversaries." While the institutional, Protestant churches of our day are in fast decline, the local church of the New Testament is still alive and working very well according to God's plan.

In the final chapters of this book we would like to share our hearts with you regarding the potential of our future if we will encourage each other and strive together for the faith. There are four priorities we must embrace if we will make a greater difference:

1. *We must express faith in God and become trailblazers once again.*
2. *We must cooperate in planting many more local churches.*
3. *We must labor together in training future pastors and leaders.*
4. *We must strive together with the same spirit of encouragement.*

Let's examine these priorities more closely.

THE TRAILBLAZERS

*"Men that have hazarded their lives for the name of our
Lord Jesus Christ."*—ACTS 15:26

From a human perspective, following Christ requires a fair amount of adventure and risk. As we stated in chapter 10, Jesus' call to "follow" was radical and left no room for sitting on the fence. The Christian journey is an invitation for us to leave our comfort zones spiritually, intellectually, and relationally. The call to Gospel ministry is a call to spiritual battle and faith-filled "risk."

Our forefathers consistently blazed a trail of pure doctrine, courageous preaching, confrontational evangelism, and effective ministry. Independent Baptists historically have not been "risk averse." We have been the chance takers and trailblazers—willing to leave denominations, willing to stand alone, and willing to try new ways of applying biblical principles to modern ministry.

A generation ago, we weren't afraid to boldly try new ideas or implement new tools in an effort to reach more souls for Christ so long as they were the implementation of biblical principles. We pioneered bus ministries, Gospel radio, broadcast preaching, Sunday schools, Open Houses, and print media. Our history is replete with men who embraced new technologies. They relished the challenge of upsetting the status quo in order to break through to a new level of effective ministry. (We've already stated our commitment to pure doctrine, so nothing in this chapter should be viewed to the detriment of biblical principles, but always under the authority of them.)

The previous seven chapters of this book have most likely challenged you to move beyond the status quo. We have invited you to lead your local church out of its comfort zone and back into the battle—aggressively, strategically, creatively, and passionately applying biblical principles to reach people and see them come to spiritual maturity in your church family.

We're not challenging you to recklessness or carelessness with "new and unproven" things, but we are challenging you to think of the the next "bus ministry" or "radio ministry." Look for any creative way to reach more people without violating biblical principles.

We don't experiment with biblical truth. We don't experiment with eternal souls. We don't experiment with final authority. But we do implement. We must understand our times, understand our commission, and then be aggressive and creative about fulfilling our purpose with biblical authenticity and strategic implementation.

To return to the biblical principles we've studied and to implement them effectively in a lost 21st century culture will require a new generation of trailblazers! And to that end we invite you to saddle up and ride!

We need not look over the fence of compromise, for the contemporary church movement is failing. In fact, its leaders have documented the failure in their own studies.[1] Their thirst for cultural conformity has led to large crowds of weekend attendees that experience little life change and live no differently than the world around them. We must not forsake the proven paths of God's Word and God's instructions for His local church. But we do need to leave our comfort zones with a fresh, faith-filled vision of duplicating the book of Acts in the information age. Not only *can* it be done—it *has* been done and *is* being done by many healthy independent Baptist churches around the world.

What will prevent us from blazing the trail forward once again? What will literally kill the forward momentum of independent Baptists? Five "fear factors." Let's take a closer look.

FEAR OF THE NEW

We are comfortable with what is familiar, and all too often, that which is unfamiliar we are quick to brand as unbiblical. This spiritual reflex is not something we want to lose—for it is rooted in caution and spiritual watchfulness. But it is something we want to temper and balance.

Those of us who have led in ministry for more than a few years naturally lean towards being cautious because we've seen the slippery slopes of compromise and how quickly biblical values can be eroded. We should appreciate the motive of this spiritual reflex to protect purity, and we should honor the heart of men—especially those older in ministry, who seek to protect us.

At the same time, our reflex can cause us to resist needful tools or strategies—not because they violate biblical principle—but merely because they are unfamiliar or new.

For instance, I (PWC) (having a good dose of this cautious mindset) have tended to be disapproving and resistant to a ministry using the internet. For many years I've heard of and dealt with the damaging results of inappropriate internet use—from chat rooms, to inappropriate forms of social networking, to gossip blogs, to pornography. Naturally, after many hours of counseling in these situations, it was hard to imagine the internet being useful for Gospel ministry. Frankly, my heart has often wanted to emerge from these counseling sessions with a sledge hammer and destroy every computer in sight—and then begin a campaign to challenge others to do the same! When you see marriages wrecked and lives ruined, you tend to gravitate quickly toward a hatred of the tools. And yet, it isn't the tools that wrought the destruction—it was the wickedness of sin and the flaws of the human heart. The tools merely revealed what was already there.

So while I still preach often against online evils, I have become much more familiar recently with the ministry opportunities afforded through websites, media streaming, podcasting, ministry blogs, and other emerging technologies. I have felt like the men a century ago must have felt about the "new fangled radio ministry." Yes, they were against it at first—not because they were stodgy old men clinging to "past glory" but because they were men of God with sensitive hearts toward the deceptiveness and subtlety of Satan.

Today, we must not lose our appreciation for men with such sensitivity and passion. In fact, we must reproduce these same qualities in the next generation of leaders. If we fail to do so, they will not be trailblazers—they will be backsliders.

Beyond the immediate caution, we must be willing to investigate possibilities and ask tough questions about the things with which we are not familiar. The critical question about something new is simply this: does the basic use of this in any way violate biblical principles? Is there a biblically consistent and helpful application? Not every new concept should be embraced, nor should every old concept be retained.

Trailblazers of local church ministry must be willing to become familiar with a new tool and then proceed to use it for God's glory. Much of what you have read in these pages may be "new" or unfamiliar to you. That does not make it wrong. It just means you should investigate and contextualize it within a biblical framework for your local church.

FEAR OF FAILURE

Good old-fashioned fear will destroy God's vision for your church. It's a scary thing to try something you've never tried before. What if it does not work? What if people don't accept it? What if it makes me look stupid? How many thousands of ideas in history failed when someone tried them?

Here is a better question: how many cities did the Apostle Paul attempt to reach where he saw little or no fruit? How many times did he have to shake the dust off of his feet and move on to the next city?

Tom Watson, the founder of IBM, referenced failure this way, "It's quite simple, really. Double your rate of failure. You're thinking of failure as the enemy of success. But it isn't at all." Failure is the building block of success. Thomas Edison literally failed thousands of times before he invented a working light bulb—and he expected to fail! In every one of those failures he learned critical lessons that eventually led to his success.

Fear of failure will absolutely prevent you from implementing many of the practices of healthy churches. Studying them and reading of their implementation in other churches is one thing—but putting them to work in your own church is another! It's risky. It's hard work. It's a chance to fall flat on your face as a leader.

Putting these practices into place will not be easy, seamless, or without hitch. You may try ten times to get a faithful soulwinning ministry going or to see an effective discipleship program operating well. You will launch out, struggle, fly for a while, and then lose momentum. At that point you will pray, tweak, rethink, retrain, and relaunch. And every time you "try again" your efforts will work better. Don't fear failure. Expect it and build on it.

FEAR OF CRITICISM

All new ideas go through three phases—rejection, tolerance, and acceptance. Every time I (PWC) have stood before our church family to propose a new ministry, a new building, or a new spiritual endeavor people have had these three responses—and many people go through all three phases.

News flash! Leaders get criticized. It's a fact of life. And if your church will do anything for God, be prepared for criticism. Don't fear it, don't ignore it, and don't let it kill God's vision.

First, we experience criticism from within. Every church family is different, but most, to some degree or another, are "set in their ways." If we will be trailblazers we must help our church family be visionary rather than sedentary. There is a natural drift toward lethargy in a local church family—and few people relish being awakened out of lethargy. Comfort zones are comfortable!

Thus, compelling people forward is sometimes met with criticism. The key phrase used at Lancaster Baptist to help our church family experience a constant spirit of forward momentum is simply this: *a growing church is always in transition.* I (PWC) have said this statement thousands of times. In fact, if I stepped into the pulpit right now and said to the church, "A growing church is…"—the church family would reflexively respond, "…always in transition!" This phrase has kept us willing to move classrooms, move pews, lose our favorite parking spot, or divide our class. We've tried to maintain a spirit of flexibility and anticipation—and this has done much to help people through the three phases of rejection, tolerance, and acceptance.

Second, we experience criticism from without. In the history of our church, we have been criticized for the most miniscule things—from the sloped floor or color scheme of our auditorium to the particular use of a technology or tool to the shape of our pulpit. Again, usually the criticism comes from men who are simply concerned and passionate for righteousness. Very little of it has been hurtful, malicious, or borne of envy or pride. I have always appreciated the sincere spirit of a godly man who will call or write me personally with concerns or questions.

Criticism is your friend. It forces you to dig deep, think carefully, and act cautiously. Where you are convinced of God's will and direction, criticism will not stop you. Where you are unsure and open to biblical counsel and admonition, criticism will open your eyes to blind spots and things you've missed.

If you will be a trailblazer, you cannot fear criticism. You may respond kindly to it, you may need to lead good people through it, and you may even have to confront it with a biblical spirit of resolution—but you can't fear it. When God is leading, don't shrink away in retreat, no matter who is shooting at you.

Romans 14:3–5 says, "Let not him that eateth despise him that eateth not; and let not him which eateth not judge him that eateth: for God hath received him. Who art thou that judgest another man's servant? to his own master he standeth or falleth. Yea, he shall be holden up: for God is able to make him stand. One man esteemeth one day above another: another esteemeth every day alike. Let every man be fully persuaded in his own mind."

FEAR OF DISCOMFORT

Some do not blaze a trail because they are content with the status quo. Like the pastor who didn't want to have a church with more than 200 people, they are stuck in a paradigm of comfort and would rather die ineffective and irrelevant than face the rigors of change to make a difference.

We cannot afford to be the modern-day equivalents of the first century Jewish Christians pushing their limited and flawed perspective on the newly converted Gentiles. We must be modern-day Apostle Pauls—pushing ourselves out of our comfort zones and having a holy discontentment with the status quo.

Philippians 3:14 says, "I press toward the mark for the prize of the high calling of God in Christ Jesus."

Applying this book to your local church will, in some ways mean discomfort, change, and awkwardness. Perhaps you have no clue how to get a decent website up and running. Perhaps the limitations of your budget and the condition of your building make positive first impressions seem beyond your reach. Perhaps the complexity of instituting systems for follow-up and discipleship seems overwhelming.

How big is your God? How big is His heart for your local church and your city? How willing are you to move beyond your comfort zone and trust Him? Trailblazers do not seek comfort—they seek revival.

FEAR OF COSTS

Risky ventures always cost. Sometimes the costs are monumental. But isn't that the heart of true Christianity? All over the world, men lie in unmarked graves because they were willing to hazard their lives for Gospel advance. Jesus describes the cost of true discipleship when he says: "So likewise, whosoever he be of you that forsaketh not all that he hath, he cannot be my disciple" (Luke 14:33). In other words, following Jesus will cost you everything.

Being a trailblazer requires that we look past the costs and see a world that needs help. It requires all of us to search our souls and utilize every opportunity to preach the Gospel—reaching the billions who need Jesus before it is too late.

Let us realize that the goal Christ sets for us is not self preservation and status enhancement, but reaching people for the glory of God. Paul made it clear in 1 Corinthians 9 that he would do anything but dishonor God to reach the lost. He taught in politically risky places—at Jewish synagogues, on Mar's Hill, and in Roman amphitheaters. He took heat from his Jewish brethren about his choice of company and his willingness to reach out to people considered unsavory and off limits. He was a trailblazer who didn't fear the costs of discipleship.

Jesus calls us to take faith-risks. In Matthew 14, we see Peter taking an enormous risk in stepping out of a boat into a violently surging sea. He was willing to follow Jesus into the dangerous unknown—something "sensible" people would have told him was crazy. Peter put himself in a position to fail, and did fail—until he was helped by Jesus. But Peter walked on water with God's help.

Jesus isn't surprised by our failures. He understands they are part of our growth process. He invites us into risky adventures where failure might be inevitable. But it is when we are sinking beneath the waves that we discover Jesus can work the miraculous through us.

So why take risks and blaze trails? Because the cost of inaction is higher than the cost of taking the risk.

SPOTLIGHTING CHURCHES THAT WORK

GRACE BAPTIST CHURCH

SOUTH CHARLOTTE, NC

In 2004, Pastor Chris Edwards followed God's leading to plant a church in a growing suburb of Charlotte, North Carolina. Chris and his wife Kristy had a one-year-old daughter and were expecting their second child. They were ministering in the dynamic Heritage Baptist Church of Woodbridge, Virginia, pastored by Chris's dad, Mike. By most expectations, Chris could have remained in a promising position at Heritage Baptist for the rest of his life. But God had a "trailblazing" call in mind for Chris's life.

In response to God's leading, the Edwards left home to blaze a trail into unfamiliar territory. They faced many personal risks in leaving home to plant a new church. Though God gave them a few families desiring to help plant a church in their area, the Edwards had no ties to Charlotte, no facility, limited equipment, a simple meeting place, no financial security, no promise of success, and little to build upon. In Chris's words, "We uprooted our family for nothing more than a dream in our hearts." But God has blessed His vision in a miraculous way!

The Edwards were strengthened by the giving of the families they began with and were also supported by the Heritage Baptist Church and a handful of other churches. This support allowed them to invest their full-time efforts into establishing a new church in this fast growing area.

Beginning in a rented community center, the church started with a few families. They began with a creative weekly service schedule—conducting classes in the restrooms, kitchen, and outdoors. Every Sunday after the 11 AM service, they hosted a lunch followed by an afternoon service at 1:30. This allowed guests (85% of them) to stay, meet the pastor's family, and also to attend the later service. This weekly fellowship and hospitality went a long

GRACE BAPTIST CONTINUED...

way toward implementing many of the principles we've discussed—inviting guests, first impressions, etc. It was often at this afternoon lunch that the Edwards led people to Christ, built strong relationships, compelled spiritual commitments, and discipled new believers.

In one year, the church reached 100 in weekly attendance—many of them new Christians. Though the Edwards had moved to the "Bible-belt," they discovered a thirst in the hearts of people for a biblically modeled local church. Chris preached strong doctrine and upheld biblical standards, but he balanced this with compassionate discipleship and grace. The Spirit of God used this biblical balance to do a great work in the hearts of people.

After their first eighteen months, the church outgrew the community center and began renting a school facility. Five years later, this young church is now averaging just under 300 every week and still taking faith-risks for the future.

From the early days, the church family began saving and praying for land. Pastor Edwards established a money-market account for the building fund and each week designated a percentage of the offering to be placed into this savings. The church family began to share the burden for a future facility, and many of them began giving designated offerings directly to the building fund. Over four years, the church saved $700,000.

Recently, God miraculously connected the church with a ten acre parcel of ground worth $960,000. By faith the church offered $750,000, and three days later the offer was accepted! Still expressing faith and taking risks, the church is now working with city planners, engineers, and architects to develop the land and eventually relocate into their own building.

The Edwards are but one example that God still blesses faith, and the local church still works! Pray for Grace Baptist Church, and pray that God will raise up a new generation of young families like the Edwards who are willing to express faith and blaze new trails!

Remember the parable of the talents in Matthew 25:14–30? Three men were given large sums of money by their boss. Two men took the risk of putting their money into the market. Both of those men turned a handsome profit. The third man buried his money, afraid of losing what he had. He did not understand that the risk of inaction was greater than the risk of failure. When the master returned, the third servant lost what he had been given to manage.

We are in a dangerous position when our goal becomes preservation instead of biblical vision.

The greatest heroes of our movement have been the riskiest sort. They lived their Christian lives with great abandon and were expended in the process. Think of Adoniram Judson, who, in the process of trying to reach Burma with the Gospel, lost two wives and endured unbelievable persecution. "Be careful," Judson said, "don't underlive your life." In the end, he reached Burma with both the Gospel and the Scriptures in their own language.

One of the Bible's greatest stories about accepting risk is found in 1 Samuel 14:6, "And Jonathan said to the young man that bare his armour, Come, and let us go over unto the garrison of these uncircumcised: it may be that the LORD will work for us: for there is no restraint to the LORD to save by many or by few."

We all like the end of the verse: God can "save by many or by few." But what about that other part: "it may be the Lord will work for us"? In other words, it might not work out, but let's at least try *something*. How we need that spirit in the local church once again! The guaranteed outcome of inaction is defeat, but if we are moving, at least we are giving God an avenue in which to work.

That is the heart of faith. God wants to see the world reached with the Gospel, but many of us are paralyzed by indifference, inaction, and fear. A visionary leader sees taking risks as the demonstration of faith. When we begin to truly live by faith, we prove that God can be trusted.

We must act. We must dare. We must engage in forward momentum once again.

We must reclaim a pioneering mindset. We must become a trailblazing movement of church planters and ground breakers. While much of America has lapsed into a post-Christian muddle, we must develop a Kingdom mindset and return to a focus on church planting.

We must identify effective ways to connect unchanging truth with our ever-changing culture. If unchurched people do not come to our church buildings, we must think of ourselves as missionaries in a foreign country and go to people where they live.

We must be willing to use technologies and methods that are not in violation of biblical wisdom and principles.

We must encourage a culture of faith. We must strengthen young leaders who try and fail, try again and fail, and eventually try again and succeed in their godly quests.

We must look to the urban areas of our society and realize that culture flows from the city to the country. The apostle Paul understood this and specifically targeted urban areas for church plants.

We must model sacrificial giving for our children. We should encourage them by our examples that treasure is to be stored in Heaven's bank and that God promises eternal rewards for sacrificial giving.

We must open our homes as centers of hospitality to lost neighbors and fellow Christians, modeling biblical charity.

We must endeavor to engage the broader culture by lighting candles, instead of cursing darkness.

We must be willing to receive the unfounded criticisms of modern-day Pharisees who would sit in judgment of a sincere and biblical effort to reach the lost.

We must think of our churches as infantry units launched in a frontal assault on the gates of Hell. Jesus expects this of His church—and promised the gates of Hell would fall before us.

We must think of ourselves as soldiers in God's great army, donning our armor and engaging sin and Satan in battle.

We must continue to dream, even when our brothers think it foolish and the outcome seems to be certain failure.

Thousands of graves—in Africa, South America, Asia, the South Pacific, and communist China—testify that God does not guarantee earthly success in all of our ventures.

We do not appeal to the impulse of heroism, the lust for adventure, the deception of self-reliance, or the need to earn God's favor. We must regain the courage and commitment of our forefathers.

Trailblazers—we need a new generation of them! Cast off the fear, and let's ride!

CHAPTER TWELVE
TAKE–AWAYS

- We need a new generation of faith-filled trailblazers to enter the ministry.

- We need aggressive implementation of the biblical pattern of local church ministry.

- To blaze a trail forward, we must overcome five fear-factors:

  Fear of the new
  Fear of failure
  Fear of criticism
  Fear of discomfort
  Fear of costs

- Early independent Baptists were trailblazers.

- We must reclaim a pioneering mindset.

CHURCH PLANTING— ADDITION OR MULTIPLICATION?

*"Then had the churches rest throughout all Judaea and
Galilee and Samaria, and were edified; and walking
in the fear of the Lord, and in the comfort of the Holy
Ghost, were multiplied."*—ACTS 9:31

Some time back, as Pastor Chappell and I (CR) were driving through
Tennessee on our way to a mission agency board meeting, we
passed a Baptist church and were dumbfounded to see that the
church had a bus stop sign for *another* Baptist church in their front yard!
We stopped and took a photo of it, and it still amuses me when I see it.

But a photo doesn't always tell the whole story. In fact, that photo
reminds us of a profound but frustrating truth: not only are there
countless places around the world that have no churches at all, but in
reality, *the United States needs thousands of new churches.* There are tens
of thousands of areas where churches should be planted—and they
wouldn't be in each others "front-yards."

Many Christians believe we already have an adequate number of
churches in the United States and that we need to focus our church-

planting efforts elsewhere. The truth, however, is that America is rapidly becoming a mission field. At the time of this writing, both *TIME* and *Newsweek* magazines featured cover stories highlighting the "rise and fall" of Christian America—citing a 10% decrease in Christian population over the past 25 years.[1]

Aubrey Malphurs said, "Essentially, what *was* a churched, supposedly Christian culture has become an unchurched, post-Christian culture. People in our culture are not anti-church; they simply view the church as irrelevant to their lives."[2]

Consider the following staggering statistics:

1. Recent research reveals there are now 195 million non-churched people in America, making America one of the four largest "unchurched" countries in the world. Only China, India, and Indonesia have larger non-churched populations.[3]

2. No county in America has a greater churched population than it did ten years ago.[4]

3. Each year 3,500 to 4,000 churches in America close their doors forever, yet only 1,100 to 1,500 new churches are started.[5]

4. Even though America has more people than ever, it has fewer churches per capita than at any time in its history. Although the number of churches in America has increased by 50% in the last century, the population has increased 300%. There are now nearly 60% fewer churches per 10,000 persons than in 1920.[6]

Number of Churches for Every 10,000 Americans[7]

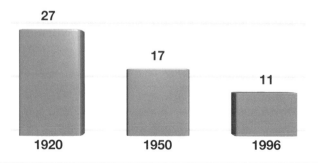

5. In a recent survey of unchurched adult Americans, 63% of Americans said they were open to being invited to church by a friend or relative.[8]

6. There are more than 1,200 communities in the western states with no independent Baptist church within a 30 mile radius.

7. Eighty percent of the American population live in metropolitan areas of more than 250,000.[9]

So, while statistically Christian-America is in decline, a majority of Americans remain open to the idea of church and Christianity! This is a revealing statistic on two counts—the fact that Christians are failing to reach friends and relatives; and the incredible hope that local churches still have to reach a majority of Americans.

When considering these stats and the fact that most independent Baptist churches average 100–200 in weekly attendees, one critical truth becomes clear—and this is a major "take-away" from this book:

America and the world need us to plant new churches in America!

At the moment, we are starting about 141 new independent Baptist churches in the United States each year. That planting rate is barely enough to replace the churches whose doors are closing forever. If we desire to make a greater difference in our nation and ultimately the mission fields of the world, we must make significant, strategic, and sustained church planting efforts a core of our strategy.

Number of New Churches Started Per Year

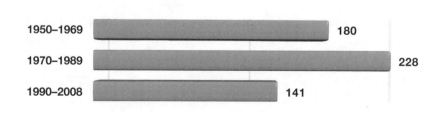

1950–1969	180
1970–1989	228
1990–2008	141

Total Number of New Churches Started

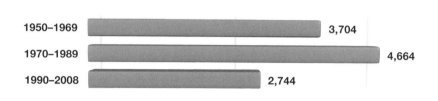

1950–1969	3,704
1970–1989	4,664
1990–2008	2,744

Much of the strategic dialogue among independent Baptist leaders has been about growing our existing churches into mega-churches. We are thankful for every mega-church that is faithful to the Bible and serves the good of independent Baptists as a whole, but the truth is that the greater need is for *more* churches. Rather than *trying* to build mega-churches, we desperately need to direct our collective efforts into planting a lot more churches in a lot more places.

Baptist history and our survey reveal that trying to *force* mega-churches is a flawed proposition. Mega-churches, since New Testament times, are obviously an act of God that stand out above the statistics as providential anomalies. God's Word and all research indicate that we would make a far more significant difference if we would strive together to plant hundreds of new churches in every state and county in our nation.

Contrast the following statistics as we compare growing our existing churches or planting new churches:

If, over the course of the next 10 years, we were able to grow 100 of our existing churches by 1,000 members, we would have a net yield of 100,000 new Christians in church.

On the other hand, if half of the independent Baptist churches endeavored to plant one other church in the next decade and grow it to 100 members, it would yield 685,000 new Christians in local churches. We would see a total of 6,850 new churches planted in the next decade!

It comes down to the difference between addition and multiplication. Our best strategy for long-term effectiveness is multiplication through new churches.

Consider the eye-opening statistics revealed by our research:

Growth Rate Comparison of When Churches Were Started

	Number of Churches	Avg. Worship 2008	Avg. Worship 2005	Growth Rate from 2005–2008	Avg. Salvations	Avg. Baptisms	Avg. Retained
Started before 1950	2,607	177	157	13%	43	16	12
Started between 1950–1969	3,704	203	174	17%	86	19	11
Started between 1970–1989	4,664	193	163	18%	70	23	14
Started between 1990–2008	2,744	141	96	47%	83	21	13
Started between 1998–2008	1,509	131	78	68%	55	18	13

STARTLING STATISTICS

Churches established since 1998, have grown at a rate of at least 68% in a three year period. Imagine the power of a 68% growth rate if it is multiplied thousands of times! On top of that, notice the number of people saved and retained in these new churches:

Number of Worship Attendees to Assimilate One New Convert

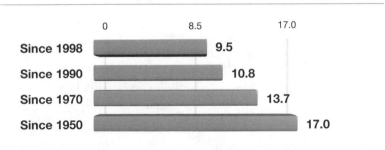

We see here, again, that younger churches grow more quickly and bear more fruit than older congregations. This principle is borne out by other research on churches across the United States: "Today, out of the approximately 350,000 churches in America, four out of five are either plateaued or declining. Many congregations enter a plateau or begin a slow decline in about their fifteenth to eighteenth year. Between 80% and 85% of the churches in America are on the down-side of this cycle. Of the 15% that are growing, 14% are growing from transfer, rather than conversion growth."[10]

In an average year, half of all existing churches will not add one new member through conversion growth.[11]

One American denomination recently found that 80% of its converts came to Christ in churches less than two years old.[12]

Churches over fifteen years old win an average of only three people to Christ per year for every 100 church members. Churches three years to fifteen years old win an average of five people to Christ per year for every 100 church members, but churches *under three years* of age win an average of *ten people* to Christ per year for every 100 church members.[13]

The bottom line is that the best growth and most effective outreach happens in the earliest days of a church plant. That is not to say older churches can't have a significant and effective growth, but the research is undeniable, and we would be wise to apply it:

Planting new churches is the single most effective methodology for reaching the world with the Gospel.

In our rich independent Baptist history, we have seen strong surges of church planting. In the '60s, '70s, and '80s, church planting boomed. I (CR) recently heard Dr. Sam Davison talk about how many of his fellow students at Bible college packed their moving trucks before commencement so they could leave to start their churches as soon as the service was over. Where has that spirit gone? Today, it seems as if everybody is looking for an established church where he can jump in with little risk. Our movement was built by faith and trailblazers—men like the Apostle Paul who said in Romans 15:20, "Yea, so have I strived to preach the gospel, not where Christ was named, lest I should build upon another man's foundation."

America needs a new generation of men who realize that there are countless places right here in America "where no other man has laid a foundation." Hundreds of cities and towns desperately need a man of vision to come start a church!

Church planting in America would only serve to increase the planting of churches worldwide through missions. In Acts 1:8 Jesus, in giving the regions where the disciples were to be witnesses, used the word *both*. He in essence said to them that while you are evangelizing your local area, you are also to be involved in the evangelization of the whole world.

Planting churches at home and abroad are not conflicting ideas. To provide the resources and manpower for planting churches worldwide, we must plant more churches in America. The *missionaries* and the *finances* for worldwide evangelization come from local churches at home, and the more healthy churches we have, the greater impact we can have around the world.

If in the next ten years each independent Baptist church planted a new church, imagine the missions efforts around the world that would flow from those new churches in the next one hundred years!

Every new church plant is potentially a *supporting* church as well as a *sending* church for new missionaries. Thus the idea of local church planting is complementary to world evangelization.

A great example of this truth is the Crossroads Baptist Church in Bailey's Crossroads, Virginia, which is pastored by Dr. Lou Baldwin. In the past twenty years this church has been responsible for planting twenty-six new churches. Annually these new churches will contribute a total of approximately 1.5 million dollars to world evangelization. In addition to the financial support, a large number of men from these churches have committed themselves to full-time Christian ministry. These men will be used of God to plant new churches. Some of them will no doubt be church planting missionaries in foreign countries.

What does the data suggest about planting churches, and what is the most effective approach to getting the job done? How can we see a rebirth of church planting in our movement? Here are a few critical conclusions:

We need to rethink how we go about establishing new churches.

Gary Walter identifies two systems of church planting: *reptilian* and *mammalian*.[14]

Reptilian systems reproduce churches by procreating as many as possible and hoping enough survive to keep the movement growing. The church planter receives little assistance, except for some financial support. Only the "fittest" survive. This serves to perpetuate the species, but it frequently leaves a trail of failed church plants and hurt, disillusioned pastors. The more hostile the culture is toward independent Baptists, the less fruitful this methodology becomes. Independent Baptists, for the most part, are presently employing this system of planting churches. In our survey, only 15% of the pastors said, "We are planting a church in which our church is the primary sponsor."

Mammalian church-planting systems, on the other hand, start churches the way mammals give birth to and raise offspring—a parent nurtures an offspring until maturity and independence is achieved. With this model, each new church would have a sponsoring church that takes responsibility for its birth by sending teams to help, investing funds, and focusing energy on establishing and sustaining this new church. This church-planting system provides more accountability as well. In mammalian church-planting systems, new churches take longer to plant, but significant support systems ensure that a higher percentage survive and thrive, making this system a better investment of resources. The key is to get the new church into "adulthood" without creating a significant dependence.

Shouldn't we, like the church at Antioch, consider sending our best people to help young churches get off the ground? This is the New Testament model. In our survey, only 11% of pastors said, "Our members volunteer at church plants," and only 17% said, "We sent out members from our church to start a church plant in the last three years."

The best, most biblical solution for reaching our nation and our world is to develop *aggressive mammalian* church planting—planting as many churches as possible with well trained men and the resources they need to get the job done. Every local church should invest itself into reproducing itself—birthing and taking responsibility for a church plant until it is self-sustaining. At that point, the mother church should repeat the process and the new church should plan to help another church plant.

We need to plant churches in major cities and towns.

We need to carefully examine where we are starting churches. Our movement seems primarily focused on rural areas in the South and Midwest—comfort zones for independent Baptists. Sadly, we have largely ignored the West, the Northeast, and populated cities.

Growth of Churches by Geographic Regions

	Number of Churches	Average Worship 2008	Average Worship 2005	Growth Rate from 2005–2008	Bus Attendance	Drive In Attendance	Percent Attendance from Bus	Average Salvations	Average Baptisms	Average Retained
All churches	13,719	180	150	20%	21	159	12%	74	20	13
Churches in northeast	1,868	150	130	15%	11	139	7%	44	13	10
Churches in midwest	4,581	156	131	19%	17	139	11%	65	15	10
Churches in west	2,465	199	172	16%	25	174	13%	68	26	15
Churches in south	4,805	195	160	22%	26	169	13%	97	23	14

Church Growth in Cities and Towns

	Number of Churches	Avg. Worship 2008	Avg. Worship 2005	Growth Rate from 2005–2008	Avg. Salvations	Avg. Baptisms	Avg. Retained
Big city (100K+)	4,482	281	243	16%	123	32	19
City (50–100K)	1,892	245	171	43%	103	29	17
Small town (<50K)	7,345	100	85	18%	37	10	8
Church plants from 1998–2008	1,509	131	78	68%	55	18	13

In the New Testament, the Holy Spirit led the Apostle Paul to focus almost exclusively on cities. Perhaps this was because culture always flows out of cities. Many independent Baptists avoid metropolitan areas because they see them as cesspools of evil or as more difficult fields in which to labor. Perhaps we shy away because of the high cost of living in these areas. Jesus, however, made it clear that His church should be engaging the "gates of hell" and promised those gates would not be able to withstand the advance of His powerful Gospel.

For the past two and a half decades, Lancaster Baptist has endeavored to fulfill this model of local church planting. While the Lord has allowed our church family to plant and cultivate several local churches in the West (including several church plants at the present) one of the "brightest spots" is the Los Angeles Baptist Church.

This church began with teams of church members from Lancaster Baptist traveling to downtown Los Angeles on the weekends for soulwinning, door-knocking, and conducting services. In the first year, the church was conducted entirely by teams of laborers from our ministry—primarily church members along with a few Bible college students.

A year into the plant, one of the dearest and most faithful men in our church—Sal Menjivar—approached me about God leading him to pastor this work. Sal was one of the most successful businessmen in our church whose business was not far from the new church. After several months of prayer and counsel, we commissioned this godly man. He sold his business and moved his family to downtown Los Angeles—where today, he pastors a thriving, indigenous, local church for God's glory.

Los Angeles Baptist Church now averages over 200 in attendance on a regular basis. They support missionaries, send students to Bible college, and are reaching the inner city with the Gospel of Christ. God's plan truly does work!

We need to cultivate a spirit of church planting in churches and Bible colleges.

Many of us have a powerful missions program in regard to the "uttermost part of the earth." But what about Jerusalem and Judea? What about the other side of town? Studies tell us that most people are unwilling to drive more than ten or fifteen minutes to attend church. That opens the doors wide for many areas!

We need to financially support church planting.

In our survey, over 42% of the responding churches said they contributed nothing to church planting. Imagine what could happen if all our churches increased their giving each year until we were investing 10% of our income to church planting in the United States! Some might argue that this new giving would impair our overseas missions effort, but in the long run, thousands of new churches would be giving to world missions. This would more than make up for whatever short-term loss was experienced!

We are urging you not to let these admonitions fall on deaf ears. When you turn the final page of this book and set it down—will it have made a difference? This is one area of tangible decision. Choose to begin allotting a portion of your outreach budget to the planting of a new church in the near future.

We need to support Bible colleges that train church planters.

We need to get behind our Bible colleges by supporting them, investing in them, sending students to them, and developing a culture in our student ministries that encourages full-time ministry.

We should ask our Bible colleges to report their current enrollments, number of graduates, and number of men who have started churches for the past five years. This will help keep the focus on sending forth laborers to establish local churches—as the New Testament pattern mandates.

We need to create loose-knit networks in various regions of the United States to work together in starting new churches.

We are not talking about creating a new "fellowship," but simply working together to start new churches. Let's say there are twenty or thirty pastors within one hour of Denver who basically agree on 99% of the issues. Why not meet once a month for the purpose of planting new churches in that desperately lost city? The network could do the following:

1. Host the meeting in different churches each time.

2. Have men looking for Bible college graduates or assistant pastors who would be ideal church planters.

3. Consider commissioning a few church members to help with the church plant. Older church members could greatly encourage a young pastor and new Christians.

4. Cooperate as a group to ensure a fantastic opening for the new congregation and provide ongoing support when needed.

5. Set aside money for funding the new work during its infancy.

Can you imagine the excitement this would generate among the churches involved? No denominational architecture is needed to do this—just a loose-knit network of churches who share common doctrinal beliefs and a common passion for church planting.

We need to establish several intermediate church planting points where Bible college graduates can get graduate-level training.

Because of our world's complexity, most 22-year-old newly married men will find it very difficult to connect with the middle-aged, middle-class residents of our cities. We also know that starting a church is vastly different than working in a mega-church connected to a Bible college, which is the only ministry experience many graduates have.

Why not identify 100 to 200 men who have successfully planted churches over the past 10 years and send our promising candidates to work as interns with them for a couple of years? Surely their prospects for succeeding as church planters would be greatly improved.

We need to have a "His Kingdom" mindset instead of a "my kingdom" mindset.

One of the reasons we don't engage in these efforts is that we are possessive of God's blessing upon our own ministries. We need to lose this mindset quickly and begin seeing the potential of broader ministry.

The best church planting models among independent Baptists are happening outside of the United States. Missionaries such as Rick Martin in the Philippines, Luis Ramos and Kevin Wynne in Mexico, and John Honeycutt in Asia are starting literally a hundred or more churches each year. As we have visited these ministries, we are fascinated by several aspects of their systems. For them, church planting is the primary endeavor. They talk about it constantly in their churches, and their works are characterized by it. Planting churches is burned into the DNA of their Bible colleges and passed on to students and graduates.

The most outstanding characteristic of their systems, however, is their emphasis that "*God's* Kingdom is more important than *my* kingdom." For instance, several of the missionaries started bus ministries in remote areas of their towns. When the bus ministry began to reach enough people, they found a young man to start a church in the section of the city where the bus route was working. In some cases, they reduced the head count at *their own* church by 50 to 75 people—something that many independent Baptists in America would have trouble swallowing.

An interesting thing happened, however. The people who were riding a bus for thirty minutes to an hour, now had a church close to their homes, and they attended with a group of people they were used to seeing. These people got more involved in the *new* church plant than they had been at the *original* church, because they now had more time and a vested interest in the success of the new church. The fact that they lived close to their church made all the difference.

Now, literally ten to fifteen new churches have been established and are growing—and the mother churches were so inspired that they grew faster themselves. Multiplication is occurring! Each of these pastors would tell you—as they let these people go, God moved in an amazing way to replace them over and over again.

This method is consistent with the biblical pattern found in Acts 13:1–3, "Now there were in the church that was at Antioch certain prophets and teachers; as Barnabas, and Simeon that was called Niger, and Lucius of Cyrene, and Manaen, which had been brought up with Herod the tetrarch, and Saul. As they ministered to the Lord, and fasted, the Holy Ghost said, Separate me Barnabas and Saul for the work whereunto I have called them. And when they had fasted and prayed, and laid their hands on them, they sent them away."

The church at Antioch sent out church planters who first went from Selucia to Cyprus to Salamis where they preached the Word of God. From there they journeyed to Paphos, Perga, and to Antioch in Pisidia. At this point they preached the Gospel to many people, and their response is shown in verses 49–52:

"And the word of the Lord was published throughout all the region. But the Jews stirred up the devout and honourable women, and the chief men of the city, and raised persecution against Paul and Barnabas, and expelled them out of their coasts. But they shook off the dust of their feet against them, and came unto Iconium. And the disciples were filled with joy, and with the Holy Ghost."

After being rejected in one city, Paul and Barnabas saw a great revival in Iconium. Chapter 14 tells of a great number of Jews and Gentiles who believed and explains that Paul and Barnabas stayed there a long time teaching and preaching the Word of God. At some point, resistance arose and they fled to Lystra, Derbe, and cities of Lycaonia where they continued to preach Christ. After being resisted and even stoned, the Apostle Paul and Barnabas continued to minister in these cities before returning back to Antioch to report on what God had done through their work. Acts 14:21–28 tells the rest of the story:

"And when they had preached the gospel to that city, and had taught many, they returned again to Lystra, and to Iconium, and Antioch, Confirming the souls of the disciples, and exhorting them to continue in the faith, and that we must through much tribulation enter into the kingdom of God. And when they had ordained them elders in every church, and had prayed with fasting, they commended them to the Lord, on whom they believed. And after they had passed throughout Pisidia, they came to Pamphylia. And when they had preached the word in Perga, they went down into Attalia: And thence sailed to Antioch, from whence they had been recommended to the grace of God for the work which they fulfilled. And when they were come, and had gathered the church together, they rehearsed all that God had done with them, and how he had opened the door of faith unto the Gentiles. And there they abode long time with the disciples."

The pattern we see in Acts 13–14 is as follows:

1. *A local church sends out church planters (13:1–3).*
2. *Church planters preach Christ to receptive areas (13:4–14:20).*
3. *Church planters disciple new converts (14:21–23).*
4. *Church planters report God's work (14:27).*

Yes—the local church still works, just as it did in the book of Acts.

Whatever you miss in this book—don't miss this. *America needs new churches!* The strength of the independent Baptist churches of America has always been our willingness to start new churches, and our new churches have proven to make a difference! This is still our strength today—it is how we are seeing the most success. However, we are planting fewer churches than we did a generation ago, and the population of our country is increasing. It is time to radically ramp up our church planting efforts. There is no doubt that God will bless this approach—He always does. The simple question is—will we obey?

CHAPTER THIRTEEN
TAKE–AWAYS

- America is one of the world's largest "unchurched" populations.

- Every year, nearly 4,000 churches in America close doors for good.

- Sixty-three percent of Americans are still open to being invited to church.

- America needs a revival of local church planting.

- Planting new churches is the most effective method of reaching people with the Gospel.

- Growing existing churches is not as effective as planting new churches.

- Strong churches must give birth to new churches.

- We must focus on major population centers.

- We must cultivate a spirit of church planting in our Bible colleges.

- We must invest in church planting.

- We must work together to plant new churches.

TRAINING FUTURE LEADERS

"For this cause left I thee in Crete, that thou shouldest set in order the things that are wanting, and ordain elders in every city, as I had appointed thee: "—TITUS 1:5

A leader wisely said, "Take the high road—but take someone with you!" All of the challenges and practices we've discussed in this book will come to naught if we fail to pass them on. We must consider everything we have studied in a context larger than our own lives and churches. What about the next generation? Are we passing along these values and practices? Are we going to hand off a biblical model of ministry?

One thing is for certain—plenty of voices are shouting for the attention of young independent Baptists. Our next generation of leaders are often found longingly looking over the fence of new evangelicalism. They don't always see the danger, and they are intrigued by the innovation. Our next generation of leaders are not looking to reject sound doctrine— but they are longing for ways to apply that doctrine to the times in which we live.

I (pwc) recently spoke to a president of a large, non-denominational, accredited Bible college who lamented the difficulty he has experienced in getting young people from the "seeker-sensitive" churches to be even remotely interested in Christian education or ministry.

In contrast, there are more independent Baptist Bible colleges with growing enrollments of ministry-bound leaders than ever before. And our churches are sending significantly more young people to Bible college and into ministry than any other group of churches in the nation. As we travel the nation, we are meeting hosts of young adults who are passionate for the Saviour and are planning to serve Him with their lives. This speaks well of our future and of the potential to plant churches—for there are great and growing graduating classes of laborers coming from our Bible colleges every year. What a joy and delight it is to see these laborers entering the harvest fields for the Saviour! What enormous potential there is to place those graduates into new churches all over the country.

One of a spiritual leader's most serious and important responsibilities is that of equipping and developing other spiritual leaders for the work—and more than ever we need to focus those efforts on developing and sending forth future ministers of the Gospel. It has been said, "It is only as we develop others around us that we permanently succeed."[1] This statement summarizes much of our ministry mandate from the Scripture.

Throughout the New Testament we see the work of the local church accomplished by teams who developed other teams. This method is God's heart for His church. We are commanded to perfect the saints for the work of the ministry in Ephesians 4:12. In Acts 6:3–5 we see the process by which the New Testament church identified, selected, and involved spiritual leaders:

"Wherefore, brethren, look ye out among you seven men of honest report, full of the Holy Ghost and wisdom, whom we may appoint over this business. But we will give ourselves continually to prayer, and to the ministry of the word. And the saying pleased the whole multitude: and they chose Stephen, a man full of faith and of the Holy Ghost, and Philip, and Prochorus, and Nicanor, and Timon, and Parmenas, and Nicolas a proselyte of Antioch:"

We must prepare future ministers by having an equipping mindset—one that is continually focused on the development and mentoring of others who will go and serve the Lord.

Pastors often ask me (PWC) about the early years of Lancaster Baptist Church. One defining trait of those early years was leadership development—in myself and in young Christian men. For the better part of a decade, I rarely spoke away from our church. I rarely attended a conference or pastors' meeting (not that I shouldn't have). And, with the exception of the first few months, I rarely did anything alone. Every chance I could, I personally involved new Christians in the work of God. Every spare moment was focused on the development of a strong core of leaders, most of whom are still the strong core of leaders in the ministry to this day.

The question is simply this—as you serve God, who are you taking with you right now?

Who are you actively mentoring? Who is sitting in your staff meetings, going soulwinning with you, spending time beside you at hospitals? What young people are learning from you? Are you reproducing and replacing yourself in the work of God? The only way for our life work to outlast us is to prepare others to carry on in our place.

Jesus did this. The Apostles did this. Paul did this. And generations of Christians since have done this. Now the responsibility rests in our hands.

Without question, the local church is the best place for spiritual leadership development, but few churches have a strategy for it, and many pastors are not actively engaged in mentoring others. Allow us to share three practical steps to prepare future leaders through your local church.

STEP ONE—SELECT THE RIGHT PEOPLE

From the earliest days of your leadership in ministry, you must seek out people with leadership potential. In many cases, these are young people growing up in your church, but often these are adults who love the Lord and have a growing desire to serve Him. This selection process requires discernment and the intentional development of relationships. It requires prayer and the leading of the Holy Spirit. In Acts 6 we see six principles that qualify a person for spiritual leadership:

The principle of proving—men who have a proven testimony in the church.

The principle of credibility—men of honest report and integrity.

The principle of spirituality—men "full of the Holy Ghost." J. Oswald Sanders wrote in *Spiritual Leadership*, "Spiritual leadership requires Spirit-filled people. Other qualities are important, to be Spirit-filled is indispensable."

The principle of wisdom—men full of wisdom.

The principle of humble service—men willing to assume a servant's role in the church.

The principle of active faith—men faithfully involved in the church body.

These are qualities of godly leadership—quite different from the secular counterparts of our culture. Godly leadership is made up of distinct qualities not found in secular management books or seminars.

A Godly Leader—

Finds strength by realizing his weakness,
Finds authority by being under authority,
Finds direction by laying down his own plans,
Finds vision by seeing the needs of others,
Finds credibility by being an example,
Finds loyalty by expressing compassion,
Finds honor by being faithful,
Finds greatness by being a servant.
—Roy Lessin

We must help prospective leaders understand the unique character qualities of a servant of Christ.

It is important to note that leadership development is not about finding prominent people or about appointing leaders to be prominent. It is about discerning spiritual qualities and developing those qualities for the service of Christ. It has been said, "Never confuse prominence with significance. If you think because you are not prominent, your ministry isn't significant, you are dead wrong."

Most likely, as you are reading this, the Holy Spirit is laying someone upon your heart that you should mentor—someone you should intentionally give time and energy to as they prepare for ministry. Act upon those promptings, and begin pouring your life and leadership into that person.

STEP TWO—IDENTIFY WITH AND MENTOR FUTURE LEADERS

Many leaders struggle with identifying with people, but leadership development requires time and connection with future leaders. We cannot afford to be too busy, too self-consumed, or too insecure to develop other leaders. Many pastors are hesitant to be transparent and approachable. This insecurity keeps them from being close to others—especially those whom they could build and prepare for service. Potential leaders are *drawn* to someone who will be real and transparent—and they easily see through insecurities and facades of leadership. They want to be developed by someone who is willing to identify and engage with them.

If there are two character traits that resound in this generation they are these: young leaders long for genuine relational connections; and young leaders see through our "mystiques." In fact, they are repelled by them. The longing for connection is seen in how rabidly this generation has embraced social networking. They long for dialogue, real connections, and real-time access to genuine friendships. For this reason, the leadership mystique of a generation ago is viewed by the next generation as arrogant and out of touch with reality.

We challenge you to be like Jesus—He identified with people. He walked among them, touched them, and spent time with them. Interaction is the very foundation of leadership development. It requires that experienced leaders personally identify with and mentor those coming behind them.

If we looked at your schedule for the last few weeks, would we see any time spent with future leaders? Would we see any opportunities that you have created to meet with, pray with, teach, and train others to serve God and lead His people? If the future leaders within your reach cannot look to you for development, to whom will they look?

At Lancaster Baptist we've chosen some special events and meetings for the express purpose of identifying with and mentoring spiritual leadership. You may choose different environments, but I would encourage you to make mentoring a part of your ministry routines.

Men's leadership training meetings. These meetings involve a meal, prayer, good fellowship, and focused spiritual leadership lessons.

Ladies' fellowships. These are focused times when the ladies of the church are developed and encouraged.

Saturday night men's prayer meeting. Consider meeting with men to pray for each other and for Sunday's services.

Men's leadership retreats. Consider taking a group of growing men away to focus on developing spiritual leadership potential.

Focused intern programs. Every local church should have an intern program for future ministry leaders. Some churches provide this during the summer months for Bible college students. Others bring on one or two interns for a year or two—primarily to help them prepare for future leadership. If half of our independent Baptist churches would train one intern next year, we would develop over 6,000 new leaders for future ministry!

Annual staff or leadership meetings. Consider having regular times of training and development for those who serve with you.

Frequent home fellowships. We've already discussed hospitality, but one significant purpose of hospitality is to mentor young people. There's something special about opening your home to future leaders—and you are teaching them a tremendous ministry practice in doing so!

Why do we mentor and disciple people? There are five worthy purposes in developing Christians to be spiritual leaders.

1. They learn the joy of a life committed to Jesus.

2. They see that real Christianity is distinct from pagan culture.

3. They realize that integrity must begin in their personal lives with God.

4. They know that fellow Christians are praying for them and are available to them.

5. They learn that God is able to do great things through surrendered people.

STEP THREE—IMPART RESPONSIBILITY TO FUTURE LEADERS

Author Ed Cole said, "Maturity does not come with age; it comes with the acceptance of responsibility." Few things will help future leaders prepare for ministry more than being handed responsibility and given the opportunity to genuinely succeed with it. This requires delegation—imparting ministry opportunities to those we are training.

Delegation frightens us. The process of finding, mentoring, and empowering others is something with which many leaders struggle. Why do we hesitate to delegate? There are two basic reasons—insecurity and disorganization. Either we are immature in letting others have responsibility, or we are not structured in our strategy of how to give responsibility.

Insecurity—Leaders who are grasping for influence feel threatened when another leader or ministry is blessed. Leaders who desire to please God feel grateful when another is blessed. These differing attitudes frequently occur *within* as well as *without* the local church. If you struggle with letting others handle responsibility, search your heart. If you envy or resent the blessings or recognition of others, or if you cling to responsibility for reasons of personal insecurity, you are greatly limiting your influence and ministry. Overcome this insecurity, and start helping others succeed. Find your success in the success of others around you.

Disorganization—Perhaps the process of leadership development just seems like hard work. It is, but it is biblical work as well. Leadership development is the work of the ministry. Please do not allow personal disorder to stand in the way of helping future leaders succeed for Christ. Don't allow disorganization to prevent others from experiencing the joy of spiritual leadership and ministry involvement. Clean up your processes, and start helping others reach their potential.

Keys to successful delegation:
1. Mentor and teach before you delegate.
2. Give clearly identifiable duties.
3. Verbalize confidence in the person.
4. Give them authority to get the job done.
5. Establish budget limits if applicable.
6. Allow them room to fail and learn from mistakes.
7. Set predetermined checkpoints for evaluation.
8. Praise them and give credit for a job well done.

As you determine to prepare to send forth laborers, here is a short list—a strategy of what areas in which to mentor:

Mentor in soulwinning. Soulwinning is always better caught than taught. Take a future leader out with you, and let him see you winning others to Christ.

Mentor in prayer. Future leaders must understand that spiritual battles are won on our knees, and they must enter the ministry with a reliance upon God.

Mentor in sound doctrine. Second Timothy 3:15–16 teaches that the doctrine of the Word of God is profitable. Our future leaders must be able to rightly handle the Word of God.

Mentor in methods. Methods involve the practical "how-to" of ministry. Equipping future leaders must be practical—we must show them how to do the work.

Every time you are with a developing leader, impart something in the way of practical, doctrinal, or spiritual understanding. Use your mentoring times deliberately and wisely.

By faith, we believe there are thousands of potential new churches that will need equipped young pastors and pastor's wives. These future pastors, right now, are attending your Sunday school classes, your Christian school, your children's ministry, and even your nurseries—this week! God is going to touch their hearts. It may be at a teen camp, a youth conference, a retreat, a revival, an adult class, or a Sunday service. It will most likely be through you. He is going to call them to serve Him with their lives.

From there, He will enable you to give them the sound biblical foundation and the practical ministry philosophy that they will need for a lifetime of faithful and fruitful service. Do you believe this? You must! Throughout thousands of independent Baptist churches in our nation, at this very moment there are future laborers in training! Consider this—if there were just two ministry-bound young people from every independent Baptist church in the next decade, over 26,000 new leaders would enter the harvest fields to serve with us! And many of our churches could send far more than two young people into the ministry.

It has been said, "To add to your church, raise up followers, but to multiply, raise up spiritual leaders." Let us increase the work of authentic multiplication!

CHAPTER FOURTEEN
TAKE–AWAYS

- God is giving us a large number of young people who desire to serve Him with their lives.

- Pastors and leaders must intentionally develop the next generation of leaders.

- We must involve young people in the ministry with us and mentor them in God's work.

- We must provide ministry opportunities for future leaders.

- We cannot afford to allow our personal insecurities to prevent us from developing leaders.

- Thousands of future leaders are attending our churches every weekend.

STRIVING TOGETHER

*"Only let your conversation be as it becometh the gospel
of Christ: that whether I come and see you, or else be
absent, I may hear of your affairs, that ye stand fast in
one spirit, with one mind striving together for the faith
of the gospel"*—PHILIPPIANS 1:27

In June of 1986, I (PWC) preached for the first time at the Lancaster Baptist Church. Terrie and I were on vacation. We had driven from Long Beach, California, to Lancaster on our way to Sequoia National Park. A friend of mine was pastoring a group of about twenty folks in Lancaster and was planning to resign. We were happy in a church in northern California and felt we were simply in Lancaster as guests. After the service, our friend asked us to step outside while he had a moment with the congregation. When he descended the stairs a few minutes later, he said, "You got the vote!" Unbeknownst to us, they had voted unanimously (12–0) to call me as the pastor!

Terrie and I were shocked! We had not come to candidate. The next day, as we drove through Sequoia, I could sense the Lord burdening my heart for the Antelope Valley. I reached across the car and took my wife's hand. I said, "Terrie, I'm sensing the Lord would have us go to Lancaster." She said she had been feeling the same burden.

A few weeks later, after moving to Lancaster by faith, I stood in the pulpit for our first Sunday night service. We had eight or nine adults in attendance. I opened the Scriptures to Philippians 1:27, "Only let your conversation be as it becometh the gospel of Christ: that whether I come and see you, or else be absent, I may hear of your affairs, that ye stand fast in one spirit, with one mind striving together for the faith of the gospel."

I shared my passion to see a church established that would stand fast in one spirit as we were yielded to the Holy Spirit. I then challenged the church family toward likemindedness as we grew together in the same Book, God's Word. Finally, I challenged them to share the vision to strive together—to work together for the Gospel's sake. I explained the concept of synergy and my belief that a local body working together can do great things for God.

Today, Philippians 1:27 is not only on the wall of the entry to our main auditorium, but it is also in the hearts of many wonderful people. As the Lord has allowed me to know and minister to thousands of pastors over the years, it has become a passion of mine to see a great host of holy men who will love God, love one another, and strive together for the Gospel.

THE DREAM IS STILL ALIVE

Recently I was asked to help form a "group" of men who would become a "fellowship." But I have no desire to organize groups in that sense. What I desire is a gathering of men by the Holy Spirit. Perhaps we will never all be in one place together this side of Heaven. But in our spirit, mind, and passion for the faith we would stand as one. I believe there are thousands of men dreaming this dream with me. They are not interested in any pettiness of the past, nor are they interested in the compromise of the present. Their passion is Christ, and making Him known. They desire to win the lost, plant churches, and train up a generation of preachers for the future who will stand in the gap.

They are passionate about missions and convinced that the local church is God's plan. As our study has shown, these men exist in great numbers in our independent Baptist churches. It is now time to strive together—to strengthen the things that remain and work together to make a greater difference.

THE SEASON IS RIPE

We are ministering in the last days. At the present, our economies are struggling. Our sons in the faith will minister in a culture that is abandoning all that is good and godly. They are called to preach in a post-modern society that has trouble defining *marriage*, cannot balance budgets, worships the creature more than the Creator, and worships sex like the pagans of the ancient Roman Empire.

The "seeker-sensitive" movement with all of its authors, mega-churches, and so-called "innovation" is failing. More than 25% of the evangelicals in the "seeker-sensitive" movement recently voted for the most liberal president we have ever had. The voting record of these Christians is only one indicator of the emptiness of doctrine and lack of convictions they have found in their places of worship. The pastors of these mega-churches can often be seen in late-night interviews or quoted in leadership magazines—but they constantly waffle on biblical issues. One day they are against gay-marriage, and the next day they are apologizing to homosexuals and back-peddling their position. When asked biblical questions of morality, they do anything they can to stay politically correct.

It appears we are repeating history:

Jeremiah 2:8, "…and they that handle the law knew me not: the pastors also transgressed against me, and the prophets prophesied by Baal, and walked after things that do not profit."

Jeremiah 10:21, "For the pastors are become brutish, and have not sought the LORD: therefore they shall not prosper, and all their flocks shall be scattered."

Jeremiah 12:10, "Many pastors have destroyed my vineyard, they have trodden my portion under foot, they have made my pleasant portion a desolate wilderness."

Jeremiah 23:1–2, "Woe be unto the pastors that destroy and scatter the sheep of my pasture! saith the LORD. Therefore thus saith the LORD God of Israel against the pastors that feed my people; Ye have scattered my flock, and driven them away, and have not visited them: behold, I will visit upon you the evil of your doings, saith the LORD."

How desperately we need the men of God referred to in Jeremiah 3:15, "And I will give you pastors according to mine heart, which shall feed you with knowledge and understanding."

Now is the time for a generation of men after God's heart! Now is the time for pastors in their latter years to remind our younger men not merely of institutional loyalty, but of doctrinal integrity, a passion for God and for souls. Now is the time to strive together—young and old, east and west—for repentance and revival in our land.

THE POTENTIAL IS REAL

Yet, with the need so great, we seem to struggle to "get our act together." Our men sometimes divide over the most embarrassing of issues. We write books and preach sermons about preferences. We are often the loudest where the Scriptures are silent, and fewer people are listening than ever before. We see attempts at marginalizing good men in a fashion not unlike the American political process.

We would never condone maligning of character or intentional marginalization in our local church, but it is apparently allowed in internet chat rooms and back room discussions with God's men. The command to strive together is not merely for the local church at Philippi. God's heart for His children in this matter is clear. Psalm 133:1 says, "Behold, how good and how pleasant it is for brethren to dwell together in unity!"

It is time to reach our potential as independent Baptists. But how?

Some would say "we have seen our day come and gone." G.B. Vick, B.R. Lakin, Lester Roloff, John Rice, Lee Roberson, Jack Hyles, and Jerry Falwell are all in Heaven. But our God is still on the throne, and it is time we learn to gaze on His glory like our earlier leaders did.

I (PWC) am reminded of a story in the March 1988 issue of *Rotarian* magazine about a wild-life organization that was offering a five-thousand-dollar bounty for every wolf that was captured alive for purposes of relocation. Sam and Jed took up the challenge and became bounty/fortune hunters. Given his and Jed's knowledge of the wolf's habitat, Sam was especially confident that they could make a mint.

They spent every day and night scouring the territory looking for wolf packs to target, but didn't make a single sighting. Exhausted after days of searching, they fell asleep late one night around their campfire. Something caused Sam to wake up out of his deep sleep. Leaning up on one elbow, he discovered that he and Jed were surrounded by about fifty growling wolves with angry eyes and bared teeth. He poked Jed with a stick and whispered, "Jed! Wake up! We're rich!"

I'm not too sure about Sam's logic—but I *love* his attitude!

How's your attitude? Have you read these pages with skepticism, sarcasm, or cynicism? If so, allow the Holy Spirit to adjust that bad spirit, and read it again. We can either be pessimistic, or we can keep our faith!

We still believe in God and in a hopeful future for His local church. And as a group, we can either be "bad-attitude Baptists," or we can pray together, work together, and make a difference for Jesus Christ.

We are not writing about seeking ecclesiastical unity with men who are violating biblical principles and doctrine. But our study reveals there are still thousands of pastors who have not bowed to Baal. Praise God! And the important issues are not our architecture, our signage, or our color schemes. We can divide over minor issues (and lose the next generation along the way)—or we can stand together and see our churches surge forward as never before.

While we are commanded to love all Christian brothers, the basis of our fellowship is the doctrine of the Word of God. Our passion is to see a striving together in spirit and work amongst men of like faith and practice. Doctrine is the glue that holds us together, and the Holy Spirit of God desires to bring unity to those who walk in truth.

SEPARATION OR FRAGMENTATION?

Our independent Baptist churches have held to the major doctrines of the Word of God, and one of them is the biblical doctrine of *separation*. Separation involves coming out from the false trends of the world and sometimes includes separating from a brother we love in the Lord. Second Corinthians 6:14 commands, "Be ye not unequally yoked together with unbelievers: for what fellowship hath righteousness with unrighteousness? and what communion hath light with darkness?" Romans 16:17, "Now I beseech you, brethren, mark them which cause divisions and offences contrary to the doctrine which ye have learned; and avoid them."

Now, having acknowledged the importance of the doctrine of separation, we must also state the importance of being honest as we deal with preferences and convictions. For example, one of the major weaknesses of the New Evangelical movement has been calling essential things nonessential. In the attempt to "tear down the walls," major doctrine is laid aside by supposed "Bible-believing Christians."

Scripturally, the eternal security of the believer is an essential Bible doctrine. The regenerating work of the Holy Spirit at salvation is essential. The doctrine of the local church and the reality of a literal Hell are essential truths we cannot "set aside."

On the other hand, one of the weaknesses of independent Baptists has been calling non-essentials, *essential*. For instance, some men include personal preferences in the "doctrine" of separation. This creates needless division with others who do not agree with the preference. Our next generation of leaders sees this needless division and tends to overreact by abandoning separation altogether. Some of our younger pastors are throwing away many vital principles of personal and ecclesiastical separation because of these imbalances. This is a dangerous trend because convictions are still the spark plugs that fire the engine of the independent Baptist church.

We must remember that we do not give account to each other in these areas of preference. Preferences within a local church should be decided among the pastor, God, and the church family—with the pastor ultimately giving account to God.

We must also realize that when we unduly exalt our preferences and opinions, the next generation of leaders sees through this. They are longing for us to call them to higher and more significant biblical issues.

The important tests of fellowship are not how your church serves coffee, how you illustrate your sermons, or whether you do or do not present seasonal dramas. Whether or not you call your physical building an auditorium, a sanctuary, or a preaching center is irrelevant—it's your preference. When we make issues of these types of things, we digress. We look foolish. Most importantly, we create a spirit that grieves God's Holy Spirit. In so doing, we undo the very work to which He has called us.

Practically speaking—it will be impossible for our churches to be what God intended and to make the difference that "salt and light" should make if we are debating minor issues.

STRIVING TOGETHER ONCE AGAIN

When I (pwc) was a young man, I would enjoy hearing great men of God preach. Then I would ask them to write their name and favorite verse in the front of my Bible. My first Bible had signatures from B. Myron Cedarholm, B.R. Lakin, Monroe Parker, John R. Rice, Bill Rice, Jerry Falwell, G.B. Vick, A.V. Henderson, Jack Hyles, and many others. As a boy I was thankful for my calling to ministry, and I could not wait to join the ranks of these men who appeared to have a common heart to reach America with the Gospel. For a period of time many of these past leaders collaborated on Sunday School curriculum, preached in city-wide meetings, and greatly encouraged each other in God's work.

I believe we must determine to strive together once again in our Lord's work while it is day. I am convinced of this fact for four basic reasons:

Our potential is great.
God has given to all of us the gift of potential. Developing and reaching that potential is our gift to God. There is still great potential for growth

in independent Baptist churches because God's Word is not bound in any age. Our survey has revealed enormous and very exciting potential!

Dr. Bobby Roberson said, "I don't have to keep the light burning; I just have to keep the bulb clean." If we will serve God with purity, He will continue to give us healthy and growing local churches across America and around the world!

Our passion is real.

Potential is never reached without godly passion. Recently in one of our evening services at Lancaster Baptist, one of our fine young men testified concerning his soon departure to the mission field. He told how he began deputation eighteen months prior and how he was now ready to leave for the field.

He said, "I have called 7,000 churches. Many times I arose at 3:00 AM so I could pray and then call pastors on the East Coast. We have traveled 94,000 miles and preached in nearly 100 churches."

This young man has great potential, but he also has a great passion to see God at work on the field of Mexico. Do you have this same kind of Holy Spirit passion to be used of God?

As we travel the country meeting independent Baptists in churches and conferences, one thing is consistent—we are a passionate group! May God fan the flames of that passion to our children's children and use us to propagate the faith powerfully for future generations.

Our preachers are authentic.

The pastors and preachers in our movement are authentic, anointed, and positioned to be greatly used of God.

Every day, bloggers, gossipers, and even so called Christian papers are trashing the character of preachers. Admittedly, there have been some "rascals" in our pulpits (and in every other group as well). But for all the negative talk, we want to say loudly—we love our independent Baptist preachers, and we are extremely grateful to stand with them.

Yes, I've (PWC) had personal disappointments with men. Men who have failed morally or changed doctrinally have caused me more than a little heartache. I've even had a few "Sauls" throw the spear of marginalization or outright criticism my way. But I will not change my position because of a few men who have messed up or who are struggling with their own issues.

Our commonality should not be the preachers we know, but the truths we hold. I won't abandon truth because of failed men and their issues. And because I am independent, and we have plenty of good meetings and fellowships nationwide, I don't have to participate with spear throwers or those who are verbally abusive or doctrinally unsound.

As I type these words, I am on an airplane traveling home from the state of North Carolina where I preached in a "Striving Together Conference." This Conference was hosted by a single independent Baptist church. It was not a fellowship or denominational meeting—just a pastor and a local church seeking to be a blessing. Yet in the past two days, I was privileged to minister to a vibrant growing church and over 200 full-time Christian workers. There was no griping, no axes to grind, and no bitter preaching. There was simply a group of men who want to make a difference for Christ. It is refreshing to see strong, separated men with hearts of love and compassion for the lost coming together all across the nation.

In addition to those pastoring currently, we have a growing number of yielded and sharp young men eager to join us in ministry. I believe on a percentage basis, we have more young men in Bible colleges actually training for full time ministry than any other group in the United States. There are not nearly enough, but every one is another life who will make a difference.

While many circles are experiencing a complete dearth of young "clergy," there is actually a momentum gaining in our churches and independent Baptist colleges that is producing hundreds of passionate young preachers annually.

By the way, these young men come from local churches where the pastor models the joy of serving and a passion for our Lord and His work. The modeling they observe is not from men in mid-life crises whose Sunday messages are more like a late-night talk show host. These young men come from churches where there is a passion for preaching, singing, and serving. There are many young men in our ranks who are not caught up in the modern trends, but who are actually very much in tune with duplicating the book of Acts in their city.

Our place in this culture is vital.

Independent Baptist churches play a vital role as salt and light in the midst of today's morally degenerate society. The liberal media and the secular politicians are convinced the day of the "religious right" is over. They are currently celebrating the demise of Christian America.

While we are thankful for conservative political movements, this book is about *God's* movement—the local church. And the local church's responsibility in culture does not change from generation to generation.

Our responsibility is clearly described in 1 Timothy 3:15, "But if I tarry long, that thou mayest know how thou oughtest to behave thyself in the house of God, which is the church of the living God, the pillar and ground of the truth."

In a day when much of the evangelical community has transferred authority from *Sola Scriptura* to *Sola Cultura*, we believe our study bears out the fact that there are pastors lifting high the truth at this very hour all across America. To be sure, we need to invest more heavily in the process of inner city church planting and some suburban areas where there are fewer independent Baptist churches. But where we *do* exist, a person could visit our churches and still hear the Gospel and a sound biblical message.

Of course, there are bad experiences as well—where the message was ill prepared, a bully pulpit was used, or an issue of divisiveness was dominant; but God has a way of dealing with those issues in His local churches.

DEALING WITH OUR ISSUES

At this point you may be thinking, "You are sure painting a rosy picture of these churches. Aren't you aware of all of the problems?" Because independent Baptists are human, of course we have our issues. Let's examine a few:

I (PWC) believe the chief problem within our churches or amongst pastors is pride. Proverbs 13:10 says, "Only by pride cometh contention: but with the well advised is wisdom."

Pride manifests itself with division over personality. The first century church experienced this same problem. In 1 Corinthians we read of those who elevated their loyalty to men above that which was scriptural. First Corinthians 3:3–4, "For ye are yet carnal: for whereas there is among you envying, and strife, and divisions, are ye not carnal, and walk as men? For while one saith, I am of Paul; and another, I am of Apollos; are ye not carnal?" Loving gratitude and biblical loyalty are completely acceptable, but division over personality is a sure sign we are missing God's plan to benefit from different types of leaders.

Dr. Curtis Hutson once wrote: "Every sincere Christian should be governed by Bible principles and not personalities or preferences." He later said, "The question should not be, 'Who's taking this position.' The question should be, 'Is this position biblical?'"[1]

It is vital that our Bible college graduates know what they believe, not because a professor said so, but because the Bible says so.

Pride manifests itself when veteran leaders see different techniques and interpret them as different values. There are tremendous dangers when we elevate our preferences to the level of theology.

Pride manifests itself in division over institutions. While there's nothing wrong with being loyal to an institution that is loyal to Scripture, we ought not to divide over institutional connections. More and more our next generation of leaders are seeing through institutional loyalty and are being drawn together by a common call to Gospel ministry. And when an institution lowers its doctrinal stand or seeks the world's approval through the compromise of biblical truth, our loyalty must stand with Scriptures.

I recall a church in Southern California averaging twenty with a 400 seat auditorium. I called the pastor to see if he would like a group of young people to come door-knocking in his area inviting people to his church. He did not want a team to come for a weekend because we were not a part of his fellowship. This type of non-cooperation will continue to hinder the Gospel unless we put it behind us.

Spurgeon once said to his students, "We are not going to see revival if we go around with our fist doubled or if we are always carrying a theological revolver in the leg of our trousers."

REFOCUSING ON BIBLICAL PRIORITIES

These truly are days when Bible-believing Baptists must strive together for the faith of the Gospel. We must pray to live peaceably with our brethren and work to advance the cause of Christ. We must direct our energies into fulfilling our biblical priorities:

1. We must engage in faithful and sound preaching. We must teach sound doctrine. Preaching is not the performance of an hour—it is the outflow of a life. If the preacher grows, the sermons grow. If our doctrine and spirit is to be right, we ourselves must be right with God.

2. We must teach biblical principles of separation. We must support our positions scripturally, rather than merely declaring what they are. And we must emphasize the need to be separated *unto* Jesus. Paul expressed this in Romans 1:1, "Paul, a servant of Jesus Christ, called to be an apostle, separated unto the gospel of God...." So often we try to develop Christian character and conduct without developing a God-centered devotion.

3. We must stay in the battle for souls. How easily we are distracted by lesser, sidelining issues. We must return with passion to the primary issue of reaching souls. All over America there are men who have a list of issues with other Christian brothers and ministries, yet they themselves are pitifully fruitless in the matter of soulwinning. Hence, while they criticize others, their own ministry is lacking that heavenly joy that comes when sinners are converted! We must discipline ourselves to keep the main thing the main thing.

4. We must stay biblically balanced in our ministry approach. Proverbs 11:1 teaches, "A false balance is abomination to the LORD: but a just weight is his delight." Many men pride themselves in one particular outward form of separation while they are lacking in another. Any time we pride ourselves in a particular standard, we are likely out of balance. Our only place for glorying is in the Cross of Jesus (Galatians 6:14).

For example, we must value our stand for conservative music with a loving spirit toward others who may slightly vary from our preference. (We are not speaking here about condoning Contemporary Christian Music or worldly music. But some positions that are debated over music are not about defending the faith as much as defending the alma mater.)

Regarding music standards, I (PWC) have heard people say, "The first thing to go in the church is the music. If the music goes—everything else goes." This statement is often true, but I have also seen ministries who have extremely conservative music and, along with it, a critical spirit or no soulwinning fervor or weak standards in other areas. Apparently you can hold good music standards and other things can still slip. We must see these imbalances and do our best to correct them.

Perhaps one missing element to all of these issues is the need to love one another. After all, the Scriptures place love high on the priority list for each of us. "Though I speak with the tongues of men and of angels, and have not charity, I am become as sounding brass, or a tinkling cymbal" (1 Corinthians 13:1).

5. We must cultivate a heart for God in our churches and schools. The Christian life is lived from the inside out. There is nothing wrong with requiring basic standards of appearance for students in our schools or leaders in our churches; but to implement these policies without teaching and mentoring people to have a heart for God will bring about rebellion or resentment. Christians in these environments ultimately feel they are conforming to something they don't believe in their own heart.

We have all heard the stories of preachers who were known for their preaching on dress related issues, only to later fail morally themselves and harm the cause of Christ. I have spoken to many of these fallen brothers, and without exception they have said that they were living something outwardly, but were starving spiritually inwardly.

Anyone can excel in a few outward standards, but it takes more than this to sustain fruit over the years. Sustained fruit is a product of a genuine walk with God.

6. We must be personable and patient with our brothers. When was the last time you reached out to befriend another pastor? When was the last time you worked with a new independent Baptist pastor on a home missions project?

Sometimes I think we are like the two friends who were out hunting. Suddenly one yelled, and the other looked up to see a grizzly charging them. The first started to frantically put on his tennis shoes, and his friend anxiously asked, "What are you doing? Don't you know you can't outrun a grizzly bear?" The friend replied, "I don't have to outrun a grizzly. I just have to outrun you!"

If you have a question or concern with another man's ministry, go to him personally. How much better it is to follow this biblical pattern than to wound each other and defame the name of Christ by hashing it out on online forums.

In addition to this, let us be patient with our brothers. There are many good men in our churches who will grow and come to stronger positions in ministry if we will encourage them. Often we cut someone off before we try to reach out and edify in a spirit of friendship.

Dr. Curtis Hutson did not at first champion the cause of the premillenial return of Christ, but godly independent Baptist leaders lovingly worked with him in his early days. He later wrote, "As the years went by and we studied more, we changed our position, and we now preach the premillenial return of Christ, as well as the resurrection of the dead. I admitted that I was wrong with some of my doctrinal teaching."[2]

7. We must remain biblical in ministry. Second Timothy 4:1–3 says, "I charge thee therefore before God, and the Lord Jesus Christ, who shall judge the quick and the dead at his appearing and his kingdom; Preach the word; be instant in season, out of season; reprove, rebuke, exhort with all longsuffering and doctrine. For the time will come when they will not endure sound doctrine; but after their own lusts shall they heap to themselves teachers, having itching ears."

How quickly our personalities or practices can seem to take priority over the Word of God. Os Guinness wrote, "The faith-world of John Wesley, Jonathan Edwards, John Jay, William Wilberforce, Hannah More, Lord Shaftesbury, Catherine Booth, Hudson Taylor, D.L. Moody, Charles Spurgeon, Oswald Chambers, Andrew Murray…is disappearing. In its place a new evangelicalism is arriving in which therapeutic self-concern overshadows knowing God, spirituality displaces theology, end-times escapism crowds out day-to-day discipleship, marketing triumphs over mission, references to opinion polls outweigh reliance on biblical exposition, concerns for power and relevance are more obvious than concern for piety and faithfulness, talk of reinventing the church has replaced prayer for revival, and the characteristic evangelical passion for missionary enterprise is overpowered by the all-consuming drive to sustain the multiple business empires of the booming evangelical subculture.

"In other words, in swapping psychology for theology in their preaching and enthroning management and marketing in their church administration, evangelicals were making the same errors as liberals had earlier."[3]

8. We must guard our spirit and walk in humility. The branch that bears the most fruit, bows the lowest to the ground. One of our great personal priorities as Christian leaders should be to walk humbly before God and allow His Holy Spirit to guide our spirits.

I (PWC) have seen men become caustic and frustrated in their spirit—to the point of ruining the spirit of their own church or family. First Peter 5:6 reminds us, "Humble yourselves therefore under the mighty hand of God, that he may exalt you in due time."

9. We must pray for our fellow pastors. J. Sidlow Baxter wrote, "Men spurn our appeals, reject our messages, oppose our arguments, despise our persons, but they are helpless against our prayers." Revelation 3:2 challenges us to "strengthen the things which remain." Prayer for one another will strengthen our remaining churches and schools.

My friend—for the cause of Jesus Christ and the desperate need of this hour, we must strive together for the faith. We must live wisely, minister passionately, encourage each other continually, and surge forward together!

Benjamin Franklin wisely said, "We must hang together, gentlemen… else, we shall most assuredly hang separately."

May God give us a spirit to strive together for the faith that we might have fruit that remains to the glory of Christ.

CHAPTER FIFTEEN
TAKE–AWAYS

- Men of God across our nation share the vision and dreams articulated in this book—God has placed it in their hearts.

- We are ministering in the last days, and our nation is ripe for revival.

- We need a fresh dose of good attitudes and godly spirits.

- We must stop dividing over minor issues and preferences.

- God has given us the same passion, strong preachers, a vital place in culture, and great potential to make a difference.

- Pride will destroy our ability to make a difference.

- We must refocus on biblical priorities of solid preaching, biblical separation, soulwinning, and ministry balance.

- We must develop genuine hearts for God.

- We must be patient with and prayerfully supportive of one another.

- We must walk in humility and sincerity.

LOCAL CHURCH STILL WORKS

"…upon this rock I will build my church; and the gates of hell shall not prevail against it. "—MATTHEW 16:18

In part one of this book we introduced the independent Baptist church movement and a thorough study that ranged across the subsets of these churches. The study was both encouraging and challenging. The lessons learned from the study simply validated that biblical patterns still work and God's promise still stands. He is still building local churches and changing lives with the power of the Gospel.

In part two of this book we highlighted seven biblical practices that healthy churches are consistently observing. They are as follows:

1. Generate guests through effective outreach.
2. Create positive first impressions.
3. Connect God's Word with hearts.
4. Follow up biblically and strategically.
5. Use effective tools and technologies.
6. Compel spiritual commitments.

7. Develop devoted disciples.

We rejoiced greatly to know of the many churches across our nation where God is growing strong Christians and developing spiritual health. We were challenged to think of what could happen in our churches and our nation if more churches would rise to biblical ministry patterns once again.

In part three of this book we've taken a look at the big picture of what could happen if we would strive together. We've seen the need for a trailblazing, faith-filled spirit. We've seen the profound impact of focusing less on the development of larger churches and more on the planting of many churches. We've seen the drastic need to train future leaders who will pastor and staff these churches. And we've examined God's challenges to us in Scripture to remain biblical but also to strive together.

IN SUMMARY

As independent Baptists, we are part of something mighty, holy, eternal, and glorious—the forward marching and momentum of the local church of Jesus Christ. Although there are many blessings and good things that God is presently doing in our churches, much work remains and an incalculable potential exists.

God's plan for local church ministry is still alive and healthy! He blesses His mandates: to go out and compel them to come in, to connect His Word to everyday life, to preach the Gospel to lost souls, to follow-up with authentic love and nurture, to use strategic tools to increase our harvest, to compel people to faith commitments, and to patiently develop devoted disciples. To those churches aggressively practicing these mandates—may we press on and strive for greater excellence and effectiveness, all the while seeking the power and filling of Almighty God. To those churches who are lacking in these practices, may these pages urge you forward by faith, and may God give patience and wisdom in addressing one area at a time as He accomplishes His work through your church.

Finally—we have big challenges, but we have a great God. In the first century, twelve men changed the world. We are more than twelve!

We have more churches than ever before—but we need each church to plant another and then another. We stand to make a far greater difference by planting new churches.

We have more Bible colleges than ever before—but we need student ministries to fill those colleges with young people on fire for God and passionate to serve Him.

We have more Bible college graduates than ever before—but we need every pastor to embrace a few future leaders on a regular basis, mentor them, train them, and prepare them for fruitful ministry in an authentic ministry setting.

We have more pastors and spiritual leaders than ever—but we need to encourage each other, pray for each other, and strive together with a right spirit toward each other.

Throughout these pages we have seen biblically, statistically, and in vivid present-day examples—*YES—the local church still works!*

The question is, will you participate passionately with the forward momentum of the local church, or will you quench it?

And that is a question we cannot answer as a group...
After all we are *independent* Baptists.

You must answer it independently.

PREFACE

1. Paul Sangster, *Doctor Sangster* (London: Epworth, 1962), 109.
2. Jon Meacham, "The Editor's Desk," *Newsweek*, December 2008.

INTRODUCTION

1. George Barna, *Revolution* (Wheaton, IL: Tyndale House, 2005).

CHAPTER ONE

1. U.S. Census Bureau, http://www.census.gov/main/www/popclock. html.
2. Wikipedia, "Demographics of the United States," http://en.wikipedia. org/wiki/Demographics_of_the_United_States#cite_note-44 (accessed May 2009).

CHAPTER TWO

1. David Olson, *The American Church in Crisis* (Grand Rapids, MI: Zondervan, 2008).
2. Obtained statistics from *Mission Handbook 2004–2006* and individual representatives of mission boards.
3. Kenneth D. Gill, Dotsey Welliver and Minnette Northcutt, *Mission Handbook 2004–2006: U.S. and Canadian Protestant Ministries Overseas*, 19th ed. (Wheaton, IL: Evangelism and Missions Information Service, 2004), 272.
4. Ibid., 85–86.

CHAPTER THREE

1. David Olson, *The American Church in Crisis*, 83.

CHAPTER FIVE

1. Wayne Zunkel, *Growing the Small Church* (Elgin, IL: David C. Cook Publishing, 1982).
2. U.S. Small Business Administration, http://www.sba.gov/smallbusinessplanner/start/pickalocation/signage/lighting.html and http://www.sba.gov/smallbusinessplanner/start/pickalocation/signage/text/why.html.
3. U.S. Small Business Administration, http://www.sba.gov/smallbusinessplanner/start/pickalocation/signage/text/understand.html
4. Thomas G. Dolan, quoting Richard Reising, "E-Curb Appeal," *Christianity Today*, November 2007, http://www.christianitytoday.com/yc/2007/novdec/4.30.html.

CHAPTER NINE

1. Mary Bellis, "The History of American Agriculture 1776–1990," http://inventors.about.com/library/inventors/blfarm1.htm.

2. Marshall and Eric McLuhan, Laws of Media (Toronto: University of Toronto Press, 1988).

3. Janet and Geoff Benge, *Clarence Jones: Mr. Radio* (Seattle, WA: YWAM Publishing, 2006), 33.

4. Megan Ogilvie, "Kids' Couch-surfing Hits New High," *The Toronto Star*, 28 May 2008, http://www.thestar.com/comment/columnists/ article/432079.

CHAPTER TWELVE

1. Greg Hawkins and Cally Parkinson, *Reveal: Where Are You?* (Barrington, IL: Willow Creek Resources, 2007).

CHAPTER THIRTEEN

1. Jon Meacham, "The End of Christian America," *Newsweek*, April 2009.

2. Aubrey Malphurs, *Planting Growing Churches for the Twenty-First Century* (Grand Rapids, MI: Baker, 1992), 27.

3. Justice Anderson, *Missiology: An Introduction to the Foundations, History and Strategies of Word Missions*, ed. John Mark Terry, Ebbie Smith, Justice Anderson (Nashville: Broadman & Holman, 1998), 243.

4. Ron Sylvia, *High Definition Church Planting* (Ocala, FL: High Definition Resources, 2004), 26.

5. Win Arn, *The Pastor's Manual for Effective Ministry* (Monrovia, CA: Church Growth, 1988), 41.

6. Bill Easum, "The Easum Report," March 2003.

7. Tom Clegg and Tim Bird, *Lost in America* (Loveland, CA: Group Publishing, 2001), 30.

8. David Roach, "Survey: Americans Open to Outreach from Churches," *LifeWay Christian Resources*, March 2009, http://www.lifeway.com/ lwc/article_main_page/0%2C1703%2CA%253D168973%2526M%25 3D201340%2C00.html.

9. Bruce McAllister, *Church Planting*, http://www.bju.edu/resources/ church-planting/.

10. Win Arn, *The Pastor's Manual for Effective Ministry* (Monrovia, CA: Church Growth, 1988), 41, 43.

11. Ron Sylvia, *High Definition Church Planting*, 27.

12. Ralph Moore, *Starting New Churches* (Ventura, CA: Regal Book, 2002), 3.

13. Brian McNichol, quoted in "Churches Die with Dignity," *Christianity Today*, 14 January 1991, 69.

14. David Olson, *The American Church in Crisis*, 148.

CHAPTER FOURTEEN

1. John C. Maxwell, *Developing the Leaders Around You* (Nashville, TN: Thomas Nelson Publishers, 1995).

CHAPTER FIFTEEN

1. Curtis Hutson, *Unnecessary Divisions Among Fundamentalists.* (Murfreesboro, TN: Sword of the Lord, 1990).

2. Ibid.

3. Os Guinness, *Prophetic Untimeliness: A Challenge to the Idol of Relevance.* (Grand Rapids, MI: Baker Books, 2003).

Visit us online

strivingtogether.com

globalchurchplanters.com

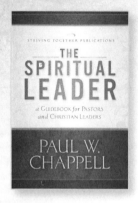
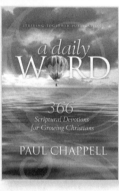
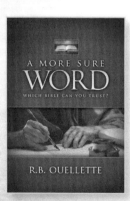

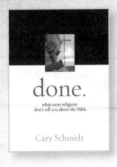
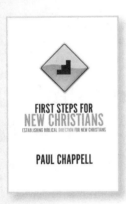

a breath of fresh air—
delivered monthly

spiritual leadership moment
a monthly downloadable lesson subscription from Dr. Paul Chappell

This subscription brings fresh ideas, encouragement, and ministry insight to your inbox every month! You receive the audio file in mp3 format, lesson outline, along with permission to use the lessons in your own ministry.

These lessons are perfect for staff meetings, lay-leadership development, or personal growth.

The monthly subscription is a $9.95 recurring monthly charge.

More than seventy past lessons are also available for $9.95 each. (Hear a sample lesson at strivingtogether.com.)

- a spiritual leadership lesson

- a lesson outline

- permission for use

- helpful staff training lessons

- personal growth helps

- bonus mp3s and mailings

- special discount offers

- annual lunch with Dr. Chappell

- $9.95 per month

subscribe today at strivingtogether.com!